Banking Certificate Series

Economics and the Banks' Role in the Economy

Geoffrey Lipscombe

Series Editor David Palfreman BA

Pitman

PITMAN PUBLISHING
128 Long Acre, London WC2E 9AN

© Geoffrey Lipscombe 1988

First published in Great Britain in 1988

British Library Cataloguing in Publication Data
Lipscombe, Geoffrey
    Economics and the banks' role in the
    economy. — (Banking certificate series).
    1. Economics 2. Banks and banking
    I. Title II. Series
    330'.024332   HB171

ISBN 0 273 02882 0

Printed and bound in Great Britain

Contents

Preface   vii

1 **What is economics and why do we study it?   1**
Introduction – A working definition – The language of
economics – How to study economics – How to enjoy
studying economics – Summary – Questions

2 **Prices and output – markets   8**
Objectives – Introduction – Demand – Supply – Price
determination; market clearing – Changing the other
influences – Elasticity: sensitivity to price changes –
Joint supply and demand – Summary – Questions

3 **Prices and output – firms and industries   28**
Objectives – Introduction – Costs – Specialisation –
Perfect competition – Market share – Oligopoly –
Monopoly – Summary – Questions

4 **Prices and output – the nation   46**
Objectives – Introduction – The general level of
prices – Gross domestic product (gdp) – The business
cycle – Unemployment of factors of production – The
role of government – Summary – Questions

5 **Banks   65**
Objectives – Introduction – Banks: the various types –
Financial markets – Interest rates – Competition
between banks – Summary – Questions

6 **Banks and their finances   85**
Objectives – Introduction – Liabilities – Assets:
liquidity v. profitability – Contingent liabilities –
Asset management – Liability management – Profit

and loss account – Intermediation in practice –
Summary – Questions

7 **Money** **103**
Objectives – Introduction – Money: a definition –
Measuring the money supply – The demand for
money – How money is created – Interest rate theory –
The role of money – Summary – Questions

8 **International trade and the balance of payments** **117**
Objectives – Introduction – Why trade? – Some
problems of international trade – The balance of
payments – The UK's recent experience – Where do
the banks fit in? – Summary – Questions

9 **Foreign exchange and related markets** **136**
Objectives – Introduction – How exchange rates are
quoted – Why do exchange rates vary? – Fixed and
floating rates – Currency baskets – Exchange rate
policy – Foreign exchange risk – Foreign currency
deposits – Summary – Questions

10 **Government** **151**
Objectives – Introduction – Fiscal policy – The
monetary counterparts – The Bank of England –
Monetary policy – Prudential regulation – Summary –
Questions

*Appendix: Economics and the Banks' Role in the
Economy* *169*
Specimen Paper 1 – Specimen Answers 1 –
Specimen Paper 2 – Specimen Answers 2

Index *177*

Preface

In many ways this book, and the syllabus it covers, is a 'quart in a pint pot', comprising basic economics and basic elements of banking. Obviously, a lot of detail on the banking side and many aspects of economics have had to be omitted. Because most students work in branch banking, the economic content has concentrated perhaps on the micro- (or branch) side rather than the macro- (or whole bank) side, in order that students may relate theory to local practice.

It is hoped that the result is still a very interesting, job-related book, which should help young bankers to understand how economics affects our daily life at home and at work. Because it is job-related and not too academic, the syllabus is suited for group learning in projects, some of which are mentioned in the questions at the end of the chapters. Examinations are lonely experiences for candidates but there is no need for learning to be a similar one-to-one relationship between teacher and student. Much of it should be a group process, so that we have the benefit of specialisation with each student researching a different part of the project, and drawing upon the wider experience of the members of the group.

I would like to thank Margaret Orchard for typing the manuscript so accurately at very short notice, David Evans for his comments on an early draft of Chapters 8 and 9, David Palfreman for advice on the typescript, and Tania Hackett and her colleagues at Pitman Publishing for their support and patience. Finally, my apologies to Jill and our children, Andrew and Clare, for neglecting them so much this summer. Without the co-operation of family and colleagues the book would never have been written. Thank you all.

1
What is economics and why do we study it?

1 Introduction

Most books on economics for students begin with a definition and this will be no exception. But definitions are barren and so, first, we need to discuss what economists study and how economics affects us all.

Economics is concerned with the production of goods and services, the distribution of these goods and services from the producer through the wholesaler and the agent to you and me, and with the exchange of goods and services, usually for money. In brief, we can say that economics deals with *production, distribution* and *exchange*.

Usually, we organise our rules and practices concerning production, distribution and exchange according to which country we live in. In the USA and other western industrialised countries (the 'first world') the system is very different from that in the USSR and many of its allies (the 'second world'). In many poorer countries in Latin America, Asia and Africa the system is different yet again; these countries have a large subsistence economy not using money and not selling their crops. This is the 'third world' about which we hear a lot from the media. Sometimes, countries come together to harmonise parts of their rules: the European Economic Community is the leading example of this type of economic grouping. The world's most important industrialised countries, including the USA, Japan, Canada, Australia and the countries of the EEC have formed the Organisation for Economic Co-operation and Development (OECD), which is a sort of club for the richer, industrialised countries.

Although the richest countries are in the Arabian Gulf, they are quite small and cannot be compared in size to the industrial giants of the USA, Japan and the EEC. Many other countries are very poor indeed – Chad is perhaps the worst example, where the inhabitants have, on average, about £2 a week each.

When we consider that some have more and that many have less, we can appreciate to some extent the rigours of life there. Just as economists study the distribution of income between individuals in one country, so they also study the differences between the average income levels of different countries.

Another topic of interest to economists is how people earn their living and what they are paid for it. Not everybody in the world earns their living from a job. Some of us are too young, too old, too ill; others work in the family as housewives; others work on the land to feed themselves and their families rather than to sell their crops or animals for cash at a market; some are self-employed, working for themselves as farmers or craftsmen rather than working for an employer; some are unemployed and long to be employed. Economists are concerned, like everybody else, with the problem of unemployment, although they often disagree as to how jobs can be created for the jobless.

But to return to a favourite subject – income, yours and mine. One half of us will earn less than the nation's average wage, and half more – for that is one meaning of an average. But most of us earn less than our bosses and nearly all of us earn less than pop stars or international footballers. Economists study the reasons for these disparities of income.

Most of us have not the ability or luck to become top-class athletes. Our physical abilities vary in much the same way as our financial resources – some are strong, others are weak. Similarly, nations differ in their natural resources: the USA, USSR, Canada, Brazil, China and Australia are richly endowed with minerals and farmlands. Japan and the UK, being much smaller in area, have fewer natural resources. But not all countries with rich natural resources are wealthy: Angola is one example of a poor country with many natural resources. Japan is an example of the converse: a wealthy country with so few natural resources that it imports nearly all of them.

2 A working definition

Resources are limited to a greater or lesser extent, but the uses to which we could conceivably put these resources are limitless. For instance, the world's food is unevenly shared by its people. In the EEC and the USA there are surpluses, while millions go hungry in Africa and other less developed regions. The world has chosen to allow some countries to have surplus stocks, while others have acute shortages. The world could conceivably alter its arrangements, so as to even out the distribution of its food. It is doubtful whether this would succeed in alleviating hunger but at least it would mean that the quality of life would be higher for more people.

Another example of resource, this time from industry, is steel. Steel can be used for bridges, for building hospitals, for pipelines and for tanks and guns. It is currently used for all of these. Economists study the way in which decisions are taken to allocate the uses of steel and to allocate the food production for consumption or for storage.

In brief, one economist, Lord Robbins, has defined economics as *the science of studying the allocation of scarce resources between competing uses.*

3 The language of economics

Economics is concerned with facts, some of which we saw in Section 1. Facts can, of course, be grouped together in large numbers and we can then use statistics to establish various relationships – e.g. the average incomes of people in different occupations. But we shan't be using very much statistics or mathematics in this book. Apart from some diagrams and some bank balance sheets, we shall be using words to communicate. We use words to communicate at work, especially to motivate people, and good bankers (as well as good economists) need to be as proficient with words as they are with figures.

However, one of the difficulties we shall soon encounter is that economists use words in somewhat special ways, like the Mad Hatter in *Alice in Wonderland*. One Swedish economist once remarked that one economist would rather use another economist's toothbrush than use that economist's definitions!

Bank staff will come across one of these conflicts very early on in their studies of economics. To bankers, *savings* is much the same as *investment* – such as high interest cheque accounts, building society deposits, unit trusts, stocks and shares, endowment policies, and pension schemes. They might say 'buying your own house is the best investment you can make'. To economists, savings and investment are very different concepts. Savings means not consuming (i.e. not using all your income to buy goods and services) while investment means the purchase of new assets such as roads, hospitals, houses, industrial and commercial plant and machinery. It does not mean the purchase of stocks and shares or any of the things it brings to the mind of bankers.

Another word much used in economics is *margin*. To business people it usually means the difference between costs and receipts – their *profit margin*. But to economists, the margin means the additional unit of sales or output, where the decision to buy a product is in the balance. For instance, if price is 40p a unit and the demand were 10 000 units at that price, the marginal unit would be unit 10 001. The marginal cost of that unit would be the addition to total costs caused by the production of that unit. As we shall see in Chapter 3, it should also be 40p under certain conditions. Elasticity is another term – as we shall see in the next chapter. However, it has nothing to do with underwear!

To be more serious, another three terms often used by economists are *land, labour* and *capital*. Together they comprise the factors of production, i.e. those goods and services used to produce other goods and services. A good example is a wood-working lathe, used to manufacture chair legs. The economist considers a lathe to be part of capital, using that term in a somewhat different sense than an accountant uses it. The accountant regards a lathe as an asset, which is on the opposite side of a balance sheet to capital.

4 How to study economics

First, do not rely entirely or even largely on memory. Obviously, it helps if you can remember facts and use them sensibly and in the right places to back up your arguments. For instance, nobody really supposes that the Bank of England's recent history if influenced much by the fact that it was founded in 1694 towards the end of the seventeenth century. More important is the fact that it is very old – nearly three hundred years – and that it has developed a wide range of functions very gradually. Again, the digits of the year when the Bank of England was founded can be shuffled round to give us the year (1946) when it was nationalised. Examiners see hundreds, if not thousands, of students' answers with this date correctly given but few ever comment that this date shows that the Bank of England was considered to be so important that it was the first private company the post-war Labour government nationalised, even before the coal industry. An economist of 1994, when the Bank will be three hundred years old, may well comment that it is still very important because it was the last asset to be privatised by the fourth Thatcher government!

Here we're allowing politics to creep in. As our definition in Section 2 stated, economics is a science, and so we must be dispassionate. We must avoid allowing our personal prejudices – such as a dislike of the EEC's agricultural policy – to affect our arguments.

We use this word 'argument' a lot because economics is concerned with choosing what to do with our scarce resources and we have to convince other people that our choices are right. Many economists are employed in an advisory capacity and they need to be able to convince their employers that their recommendations are sound and will be beneficial to the firm or government department for which they work. A list of unrelated facts would be useless.

We do not want to stress the point of avoiding memory work too much, but nobody ever learnt to swim or ride a bicycle by using their memories. We learn by practising until we are proficient; similarly with economics, which should be regarded as a way of analysing problems, such as prices, output, unemployment, poverty. In banking the two most studied economic problems are interest rates and exchange rates, which are also of increasing concern to our large company customers.

5 How to enjoy studying economics

First, regard it as a way of thinking. For instance, study the price of petrol, and who sells it in your town or village. Where is it sold? Have any garages closed recently? If so, can you find out why they closed? Closures could be difficult to explain, because the numbers of cars on the roads are still rising. Thus, relating the local market for petrol, for example, to the concepts to be studied in the next two chapters should help you see economics not as an abstract set of theories learnt parrot-fashion but as a live subject of vital importance to you and your friends.

Second, always try to relate what is in the book or in your class notes to everyday life – at home, in the bank (remember the rules about confidentiality, however) and in the High Street. We shall discuss in Chapter 4 a difficult concept called gross domestic product which is the total output of a country but it is possible to imagine the gross domestic product of a country by just driving through much of it – and we have all driven through parts of the UK! The world famous economist Milton Friedman once remarked that, having driven across England, he was amazed at how high the gross domestic product seemed to be! If he can do it, just by using his eyes, so can we!

Summary

1 Economics deals with the problems of production, distribution and exchange.
2 It may be defined as the study of how scarce resources are allocated by different countries to the unlimited uses to which they can be put.
3 It is also a way of analysing problems.
4 It has a vocabulary of its own; it often uses words in a different sense to their everyday meanings.
5 Studying economics is much more than memory-work and involves a great deal of reasoning.

Questions

Some of the following questions can be answered with a 'yes' or 'no'; others require more lengthy answers, while some are best tackled by groups of students working together and others will need a little research. They are designed not just to test your memories but to set you thinking about the High Street and the industrial estate, about our customers' problems and the banks' problems.

Answer 'yes' or 'no' to the first five questions.

I am studying economics because
   1 I have to.
   2 I want to obtain my Banking Certificate.
   3 It's one of the subjects for the Banking Certificate. It seems difficult but with good textbooks and a good teacher I hope to learn more about it and pass the examination.
   4 It's in the syllabus for my Banking Certificate to help me understand how prices are determined, how firms compete, how governments intervene to control inflation and reduce unemployment.

5 It's vital for all bankers to know about prices, output, jobs, interest rates and exchange rates.

6 Which of the following is regarded as investment by a banker and by an economist:

(a) the purchase of shares in the privatisation of a nationalised industry?

(b) the purchase of a new house (not an existing house)?

7 Name some of the member countries of the OECD.

8 What does the term 'third world' mean?

9 Explain, in ordinary language, the economist's meaning of the word 'margin'.

10 Explain how business people use the word 'margin'.

11 Why was the Bank of England the first privately-owned company to be nationalised after the end of the second world war?

12 Name some of the world's richest countries.

13 Name some of the world's poorest countries.

14 Why does Japan import so many raw materials?

15 Name the member countries of the European Economic Community.

16 What is understood by the term 'distribution'?

17 What are stated in the chapter as being the two most studied economic problems which concern banks?

18 Do these problems also concern our customers?

19 How do economists define 'savings'?

20 Explain in a few words the meaning of the term 'gross domestic product'.

2
Prices and output – markets

1 Objectives

When you have studied this chapter you should be able to:

1 understand how prices of goods and services (and also the amounts bought and sold) are determined;

2 know the major influences on prices;

3 appreciate the effect of changes in price on these influences;

4 relate such influences as population changes and rising incomes to the products (loans and services) sold by your branch and to those sold by your customers;

5 appreciate the importance of total revenue as well as of price to sellers and of total expenditure and price to buyers.

2 Introduction

When economists talk about demand, they mean *effective demand*, i.e. wants backed up by the financial ability to buy the goods and services desired. Many of us might want a Rolls Royce or a private swimming pool, but we can't afford them, so we shall never have them. Many starving people in Ethiopia need food desperately but they can't afford to buy anything, so they will die. Thus, neither the greed to own a Rolls nor the need of the Ethiopians are the same as demand.

Economists also talk about *supply* and *demand*. It seems better to discuss demand first because some bright business person will always try to supply goods or services which one or two people demand.

We can define *markets* as places where buying and/or selling takes place.

Hence, the first section of this chapter will examine demand (using the concept of the margin), then supply, and move on to show how both interact to determine price. Then, having examined all the non-price factors which influence demand and supply, we then go on to see how demand and supply respond to changes in price (i.e. their price elasticity).

3 Demand

Our wants are unlimited, but our capacity to demand the goods and services is limited by our financial resources and physical characteristics. Salt is very cheap but we need very little of it – too much will ruin our meals and our health. Hence, we don't spend much of our money on salt, although it is so cheap. Caviar is very expensive and so most of us can afford to have it only rarely. Once again, not much of our money is spent on caviar, but for a different reason.

This identifies two things which influence demand for a good or service – *price* and *physical attribute*. Price is crucial and we shall return to it in the next section.

3.1 Diminishing marginal utility and other influences

A third influence is the fact that the second 'bite of an apple' is often not as good as the first, and the twentieth may be too much for us. Economists call this tendency *the law of diminishing marginal utility*, which states that the extra units consumed of any good or service usually yield less and less satisfaction (or utility, as economists term it). To give an example of how this principle affects a service, we all need to go to the hairdresser from time to time, but only a film or TV star needs to go to one every day before going in front of the cameras. The principle is extremely important, with the notable exceptions of addictive goods such as drugs and alcohol.

Income is a fourth influence determining demand. As people's incomes have risen in the UK (and other western countries) in the past 40-odd years, so we can afford not only one car per family but in many families two cars. But in famine-plagued Africa, incomes are falling and people have to walk hundreds of miles just for food and water.

Habit or *custom* is a fifth influence – and beverages are a good example. Coffee is the customary hot drink of the USA and continental Europe; tea is a customary hot drink of the UK and, importantly, of India. But the population of India is growing far more rapidly than the UK's, which until 1983 had been virtually stationary, and the Indian government places restrictions on the export of tea from time to time in order to satisfy the needs of its own people for tea. Closely allied to habit is *fashion*. A British pram is different from a German one; elderly German ladies wear hats which no English lady would wear.

There is a sixth influence: *population*. To give an example from the UK: East Anglia is one of the few areas whose population is rising substantially, with the result that demand for roads, houses and services is rising.

Another 'demographic' influence (i.e. to do with population) is the *age distribution*. From 1964 until 1983 in general, the number of children born each year tended to fall, so that the demand for school teachers has fallen. But the numbers of elderly people have risen, and enterprising business people have created new products to help the elderly – such as sheltered housing and battery-powered tricycles for use on the pavement.

A final, eighth, influence is the *price of other commodities*. For instance, a sharp rise in coffee prices could cause some people to switch to drinking tea – a situation where the products compete with each other. On the other hand, a sharp rise in potato prices could cause the price of fish and chips to rise and this could lead to a decrease in demand from friers for fish.

3.2 Demand curves

But, of all these factors, price is crucial, so economists 'keep them all unchanged', except for price, in order to see how demand is affected by price. They then list the various prices in a schedule showing against each price the total units which will be demanded at that price.

A typical example of a demand schedule is shown in Table 2.1.

These figures can be plotted on a graph (*see* Fig. 2.1). Price is shown on the vertical scale (remember price usually goes *up*!) and quantity on the horizontal scale (remember output has to be moved *along* the ground).

In Fig. 2.1, only two things change – the price of the good and the quantity of the good. Everything else – such as tastes, income and other prices – remains constant. Later we shall see how we take into account changes in these other influences.

Table 2.1

Price per gallon	Quantity of petrol demanded
150p	62m gallons
160	59
170	56
180	54
190	52
200	50
210	49
220	48
230	47
240	46
250	45

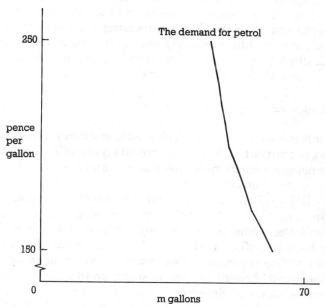

Fig. 2.1

4 Supply

Economists define supply as *the quantities of a good or service which people are willing to sell at various prices.* As well as price, technology is an important influence in determining the quantities offered for sale.

At low prices, only the cheapest goods will be offered and the suppliers with the most efficient technology should be able to offer their goods very cheaply. As price rises, so other and dearer producers find it possible to enter the market and sell their production. So, price rises should cause an increase in the quantity supplied but producers may find their costs rising more rapidly than before. This phenomenon is called the law of *diminishing marginal returns* and is as important to supply as diminishing marginal utility is to demand.

4.1 Diminishing marginal returns

The best example of this law is the old school-child poser – if it takes 12 men a week to build a house then how long would it take 36 men to build the house? Arithmetic says $7 \times \frac{12}{36}$ days = $2\frac{1}{3}$ days, but common sense should tell us that the 36 men would get in each other's way and that trebling the number of men might effectively reduce building time to 5 days. In other words, the 30th–36th men add very little to the marginal product and certainly far less than the 13th man.

4.2 Taxation of goods

Other influences, apart from price and marginal productivity, include government action. Governments quite often tax goods – such as petrol, tobacco, new motor cars – and also levy taxes on the sale of many goods.

In the UK VAT (value added tax) is levied on many items, e.g. telephone calls and certain bank services, at a standard rate of 15%. Moreover, some goods need to be imported and hence may have to bear a tariff on their price. Banks have not always been forgotten by the tax man – it was only in 1971 that the government abolished a small tax on cheques, and in some countries there is a tax on bank interest charged on loans.

Students often become confused as to how to show the effect of taxes on goods on the supply and demand diagrams for these goods and, to avoid this confusion, we will introduce tax as an element in the supply schedule now (*see* Table 2.2).

4.3 Supply curves

From Table 2.2 we can draw two supply curves, one before tax and one after tax is imposed.

Table 2.2 Supply schedule of petrol

£ per gallon	Tax per gallon	Total price	m gallons supplied
.50	£1.00	£1.50	20
.60	1.00	1.60	22
.70	1.00	1.70	25
.80	1.00	1.80	30
.90	1.00	1.90	40
1.00	1.00	2.00	50
1.10	1.00	2.10	60

We can see in Fig. 2.2 that the tax raises the supply curve upwards. For our purposes, because we buy petrol from the pumps, we shall concentrate on the top line, which includes tax.

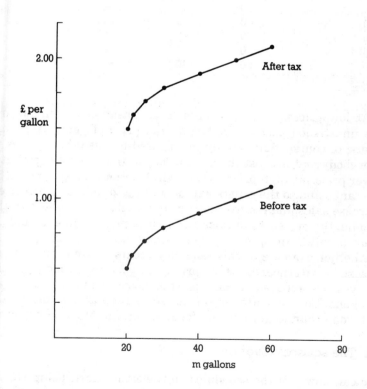

Fig. 2.2

5 Price determination; market clearing

If we place the demand and supply schedules side by side, we can show, by simple subtraction, how many surplus goods will be left unsold at each price and also how much unsatisfied demand there will be at lower prices. Table 2.3 shows the tax-inclusive supply schedule alongside the demand schedule.

Table 2.3 Supply and demand for petrol

Price (inc tax) (£ per gal)	Supplied	Demanded (m gals)	Excess demand (−) Excess supply (+)
1.50	20	62	−42
1.60	22	59	−37
1.70	25	56	−31
1.80	30	54	−24
1.90	40	52	−12
2.00	50	50	−
2.10	60	49	+11
2.20	70	48	+22
2.30	80	47	+33
2.40	90	46	+44
2.50	100	45	+55

At low prices, there will be a large unsatisfied demand and the unsatisfied people will bid up the price of petrol: the suppliers, of course, will be only too pleased to raise their prices to everybody and not just those unlucky not to have got petrol at a lower price. At high prices, there will be a lot of unsold petrol in the tanks and so the sellers will be willing to reduce their prices, increase sales and reduce their unsold stocks. Somewhere in the middle, the pressures to raise and reduce prices will even out, at what is called an *equilibrium* or *market-clearing price*.

Another example of this tendency occurs in supermarkets on Saturday afternoons, when prices of perishable food on the shelves are reduced. Otherwise the goods would rot over the weekend. So it is better to sell for something at 3.45 pm on the Saturday than to get nothing for them on the Monday morning.

5.1 The scissors diagram

We can now plot the schedules on the same chart, using DD for demand and SS for supply (inc tax). (*See* Fig. 2.3.)

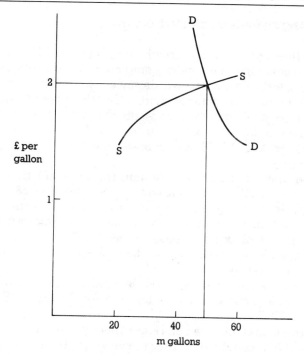

Fig. 2.3

At the equilibrium price of £2.00 a gallon, there is neither excess demand nor excess supply; the market is cleared. Diagrams like Fig. 2.3 are sometimes called a 'scissors' diagram, because many have smooth demand and supply curves shaped like the blades of a pair of scissors (*see* Fig. 2.4).

Now, in order to introduce more reality into the theory, we must begin to vary those other influences which have remained constant until now.

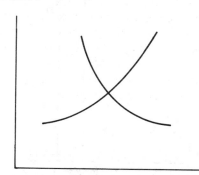

Fig. 2.4

6 Changing the other influences

These include tastes, other prices and income on the demand side; and technology and government actions on the supply side. When these influences alter, we simply construct another schedule (be it demand or supply) and draw the appropriate new curve. But, remember, taxes on goods and services change the supply schedule and the supply curve, which is why we showed two of them in Fig. 2.2. Many students go wrong and change the demand curve.

Suppose that all other prices remain the same but that we all get a 4 per cent rise in our incomes. This means we can decide whether to spend or save all or part of this extra income and it may well be that we all decide to do some more motoring. The demand for petrol will increase at each price on the supply schedule and so the new curve will be to the right of the old one. But what will happen to the supply?

Let's plot the three curves: two demand curves – one before the extra income and one after – and the supply curve. (*See* Fig. 2.5.)

DD is the demand curve before our increase in income.

D_1D_1 is the demand curve after our increase in income, and at

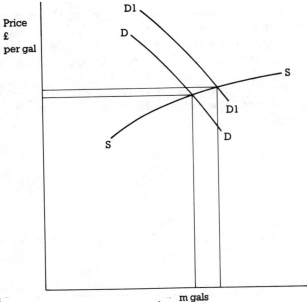

Fig. 2.5

every price (on the vertical axis) we demand more petrol (on the horizontal axis).

SS is our old friend, the unchanged supply curve.

As a result of the increase in demand, and with the unchanged supply curve, the price rises only slightly to choke off some of the new demand, but the quantity supplied rises much more, so that we actually buy perhaps 6 per cent more petrol (in gallons) for perhaps a 1 per cent rise in price.

Now let's vary another influence – taxation. Suppose the government increases the tax on petrol from £1 a gallon to £1.30 a gallon. Table 2.4 shows the new supply schedule (remember taxation affects supply). Bear in mind that the underlying before-tax supply schedule is unchanged.

Table 2.4 Supply schedule of petrol

Cost to producer per gallon	Tax per gallon	Total price	Supplied (m gals)	Demanded	Excess demand (−) Excess supply (+)
50p	130p	180p	20	54	−34
60	130	190	22	52	−30
70	130	200	25	50	−25
80	130	210	30	49	−19
90	130	220	40	48	−8
100	130	230	50	47	+3
110	130	240	60	46	+14

It seems that the new price will be somewhere just below 230p a gallon, perhaps 227 or 228p. At such a price, there should be no excess demand and no excess supply.

6.1 Shifting the curves

However, we can discover many more interesting things by using a diagram (*see* Fig. 2.6).

Shifts in supply
Here we see that the shift in the supply curve from SS to S_1S_1 caused by the extra 30p charged in tax to the producers has resulted in only a small fall in the gallons of petrol sold at the pumps, from 50m gallons to about 47.3m, but that the price has shot up from 200p a gallon to about 228p.

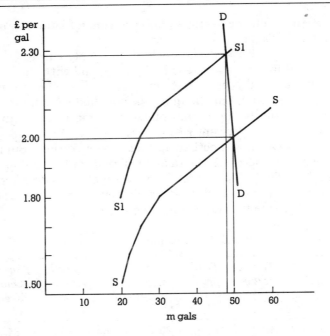

Fig. 2.6

We can now calculate the tax receipts before and after the tax rise. At a tax of 100p a gallon, the government received £50m (£1 × 50m gallons) but at 130p a gallon it received £61.490m (£1.30 × 47.3m gallons). It was worth its while imposing the tax, because it got £11.49m more in tax from us.

Now let's see what happens when the demand curve is a lot less steep than this one, as in Fig. 2.7.

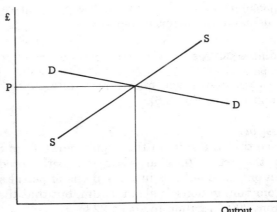

Fig. 2.7

Now let's put a tax on it! Figure 2.8 shows what happens.

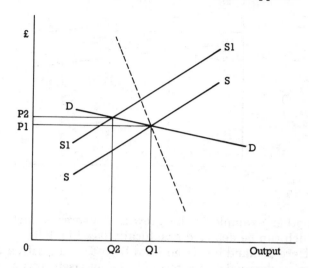

Fig. 2.8

Price rises, but the quantity sold (and bought) falls more, relatively, so that the government will still gain revenue from the tax, but not as much as it might have wished, because the quantity sold fell so drastically. The effect of the tax has been to reduce our consumption of the good markedly from Q_1 to Q_2, with a less pronounced rise in price from P_1 to P_2. The total outlay (or sales revenue), measured by multiplying price times output, which was the rectangle $0Q_1 \times 0P_1$, has actually fallen to $0P_2 \times 0Q_2$.

From the government's point of view, they still get the tax per unit they wanted (the distance between the two supply curves) but the number of units taxed has fallen from Q_1 to Q_2.

In the diagram, there is a dotted demand curve with a much steeper slope and which in many places is much more inelastic than the continuous demand curve. If this dotted demand curve were used, then the tax would cause the price to rise considerably and the output to fall only slightly, with the result that the government would receive much more in tax revenue.

Shifts in demand
Quite often demand shifts. The increasing use of ball point pens has meant that the demand for pen nibs withered away in the 1950s and that the demand for fountain pens is much reduced.

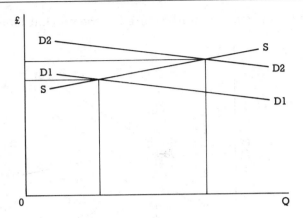

Fig. 2.9

Another example is the growth of overseas package holidays, which can be depicted graphically (*see* Fig. 2.9).

Here demand has risen from D_1 to D_2 but, with a fairly gentle sloping demand curve, prices have not risen substantially and so the output (the total number of holidays enjoyed) has risen dramatically. This brings us to a concept which is crucial in understanding the relationship between price and output, i.e. *elasticity*.

7 Elasticity: sensitivity to price changes

You will remember that in the previous section we mentioned total revenue (or total outlay), measured by multiplying price by the units sold at that price. Graphically, we show it by the rectangles between the demand or supply curve and the two axes in Fig. 2.10.

Note that we refer to revenue, not sales. We know that usually a price rise causes sales to fall (and supply to rise) but it is not so clear as to the effect on total revenue, because each case must be examined individually (*see* Fig. 2.10 (b)).

Let's take a steeply sloping demand curve and draw two total revenue rectangles (*see* Fig. 2.11).

To make it realistic we'll discuss it in terms of price rises – for falls you just reverse the arguments. A rise in price from P_1 to P_2 will cause demand to fall (it almost invariably does) but, with this shaped demand curve, demand does not fall all that much,

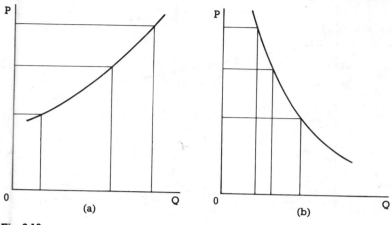

Fig. 2.10

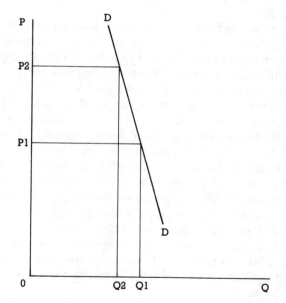

Fig. 2.11

so that it is apparent from Fig. 2.11 that the box showing total revenue (outlay) at the higher price is very much larger than the total revenue (outlay) at the lower price. In everyday language the price rise frightened few customers away.

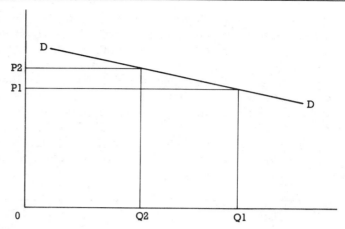

Fig. 2.12

Now let's have a look at a more gently sloping demand curve in Fig. 2.12.

Here a price rise from P_1 to P_2 has caused a massive reduction in sales (by nearly 50 per cent) to Q_2, so that total revenue (outlay) is smaller at the higher price. In everyday language, the price rise frightened almost half the customers away.

But economists prefer to be more precise and they have conceived the concept of *elasticity*: when total revenue is greater at the higher price, demand is said to be *inelastic*; when total revenue is greater at the lower price, demand is said to be *elastic*. If total revenue is unchanged between the two prices, demand is said to be *unitary*. To sum up: elasticity of demand shows whether total revenue (outlay) is greater or smaller following a price change. It measures the sensitivity of output to changes in price or, less frequently, of price to changes in output. For instance, if there is a sudden flood of goods supplied to a market then if demand is elastic there will not be a substantial fall in price. But if demand is inelastic then the price will fall drastically and certainly by more than the percentage rise in supply.

7.1 Measuring elasticity

It can be cumbersome to calculate total revenue each time price changes, so a rule-of-thumb is to use the percentage changes in price and output, and to remember that a fall in price usually causes a rise in sales. If a one per cent change in price leads to a more than one per cent change in sales then demand is said to be elastic; if a one per cent change in price leads to an exactly one per cent change in sales then demand is said to be of unit elasticity; if a one per cent change in price leads to a less than one per cent change in sales then demand is said to be inelastic. If total revenue is (say) £100m and price £100 so that sales are 1m, and a one per cent fall in price from £100 to £99 leads to a two per cent rise in sales, demand is said to be elastic: total revenue rises to £99 × 1 020 000, which is £100.98m. Total revenue is £980 000 higher at the lower price, so demand is elastic.

7.2 Practical examples

All business people have an instinctive feeling for the elasticity of demand for their products: they may not be able to express it in numbers but they have a gut reaction as to how far they can push up their prices. Sometimes they may be able to increase advertising or even improve their product at the same time, so as to mask the effect of the price rise. For instance, a motor car manufacturer may introduce car radios as standard accessories to the basic models of his cars, in order to soften the effect of a price increase.

Governments also have a need to take elasticities into effect. The first instance is when they are considering *tax changes* on various commodities – in particular the taxes on tobacco and alcohol – as we saw above. Second, governments must assess the elasticities of demand and supply when considering whether to make *changes in the exchange rates* of their currencies, as we shall see in Chapter 9.

Third, governments have to consider elasticities when considering whether or not to impose a *tariff* on a commodity. In the case of the UK, tariffs are now handled by the European Commission in Brussels and so it is the 'Eurocrats' who have to consider the elasticities.

Bankers have to consider elasticities in connection with pricing decisions for such products (services) as taxation calculations, administration of trusts, travellers cheques, etc.

7.3 Other elasticities

There are other forms of elasticity. Of these, the most important to a banker is *interest elasticity of demand*, i.e. the sensitivity of the demand for a good or service to changes not in its own price but to changes in the rate of interest. Export finance is particularly sensitive to interest rate changes, for a rise in the rate of interest might well turn a particular export transaction from being slightly profitable into making a small loss. But, for most of us, the supreme example is the demand to buy houses. A rise in interest rates could, to use journalese, choke off the demand for houses.

Income elasticity of demand is also very important. As our incomes rise, after allowing for inflation, our expenditure on such items as overseas holidays, hifis and videos, compact discs, camrecorders, dishwashers, etc. tends to rise faster than our incomes. This is important to the manufacturers and importers of such products and to banks (who can provide us with the finance with which to buy them).

Cross elasticity of demand is another variant. An example is fish and chips. If the price of fish were to rise sharply (perhaps because the fish have moved away from their usual part of the sea) then the rise in price could affect the sales of potatoes to be used as chips. The demand for such potatoes could well fall.

Elasticity of supply is measured by the percentage increase in the amount supplied divided by the percentage rise in price.

8 Joint supply and demand

This brings us to those goods and services which are demanded or supplied jointly. Fish and chips are an example of joint demand, mutton and wool are an example of joint supply. However, we are no longer living in an agricultural society and better examples of joint supply are to be found in the many products produced by modern oil refineries, ranging from kerosene for aviation fuel to heavy heating oils.

In banking and finance, perhaps the best examples of joint demand are connected with insurance. If you buy a house you need to insure it; if you buy a car you must insure it. Because banks and finance companies are very flexible, at least when compared to a manufacturer, they can quickly adapt and jointly supply the products (services) needed. Thus, home loans and the insurance for structure and contents can be sold together, as can a personal loan for a car and car insurance. Another example is travel insurance and travellers cheques/foreign currency.

Summary

1 Demand is not just need or greed; it must be backed by purchasing power. Our need for most goods diminishes as we have more of them, so that we usually only buy more of them because their price falls (i.e. we sacrifice fewer other goods for them). In brief, demand is determined principally by utility and price.

2 Supply is determined by cost and price. Costs can fall at first (as we shall see in the next chapter) but eventually they rise in line with rising output.

3 Price brings supply and demand into balance: the equilibrium price will clear the market of excess supply or demand. If price rises above equilibrium levels demand will fall away and supply will rise.

4 Elasticity measures how supply and demand are affected by price – not the broad change (up or down) but the extent of that change.

5 With modern technology many products are produced jointly as part of one process, e.g. oil refining. With modern marketing and financial sophistication, other goods and services are demanded jointly, e.g. a motor car usually needs insurance and a loan, so astute business people sell these services jointly with the car. Similar considerations apply to the purchase of houses, which is why estate agencies are being bought by banks, insurance companies and building societies, who supply the finance for house purchase.

Questions

1 Why do supermarkets often sell some goods cheaply at 3.30 pm on a Saturday? What sort of goods have their prices reduced?

2 If vast quantities of oil are discovered in, say, the Sahara desert, and if the oil can be sold on the world's markets, what is likely to happen to the price of crude oil?

3 Name some goods and services with a low income elasticity of demand.

4 If the price of oil were to rise to $60 a barrel, why would you expect oil fields to be brought on stream on the mainland of the UK?

5 Which is correct, (a) or (b)?
Sales fall when price rises because:
    (a) demand is elastic
    (b) the demand curve slopes downward from left to right.

6 You and a colleague are discussing the branch's sales of travellers cheques last year, after a twenty per cent rise in

commission charges on 1 January. He/she comments '... the number of travellers cheques issued fell by ten per cent because demand was elastic ...' *Was* demand really elastic?

7 Which of the following goods/services might enjoy an increase in their demand as a result of a rise in average incomes?
  (a) large cars;
  (b) small cars;
  (c) summer holidays abroad;
  (d) mini-holidays in the UK;
  (e) winter holidays in the UK;
  (f) butter;
  (g) polyunsaturated margarine;
  (h) alcohol;
  (i) petrol;
  (j) bus journeys;
  (k) dishwashers;
  (l) launderettes.

8 What bank products (if any) are involved with the purchase of the items mentioned in Question 7?

9 Why does a can of fizzy drink sell for 50p to tourists in the West End and yet it can be obtained for perhaps 15p in a 'cash and carry'?

10 In what sense do you, as bank employees, sell your services to your employers?

11 How many employers likely to purchase your services as a bank clerk are there in:
  (a) the Scilly Isles
  (b) Jersey, Guernsey and the Isle of Man
  (c) a large city such as Birmingham
  (d) the City of London?

12 Why do governments try to impose taxes on goods with an inelastic demand and supply?

13 If you were an inhabitant of a country with one major product – such as Zambia (copper) or Mauritius (sugar) – and demand for it was inelastic, would you favour exporting as much of it as possible? How would you attempt to maximise total export revenues from such products?

14 It is suggested that the EEC may require the UK to impose VAT at 15 per cent on new construction work. If this tax of 15 per cent were levied on new houses, what effect is it likely to have on the prices of existing houses? What are likely to be its effects on the demand for the following bank products:
  (a) home loans?

(b) insurance (structure)?

(c) income from estate agency subsidiaries, which is a percentage of the price of houses?

15 Why do banks usually lend only about 50 per cent of the value of unprocessed commodities with an inelastic demand but a higher percentage of the value of manufactured goods which have a more elastic demand?

16 Assess the influence of first, fashion and second, custom/habit on the demand for these bank products:

(a) non-interest bearing current accounts;

(b) unit trusts.

17 Why do restaurants on top of mountains charge sky-high prices for meals and drinks?

18 What bank products are likely to be sold by banks in towns such as Worthing, Eastbourne and Rhyl, where many customers are retired?

19 What bank products are likely to be sold by banks in new towns and suburbs with a high proportion of 'young marrieds'?

20 Which bank products serve the relatives of dead people?

3
Prices and output – firms and industries

1 Objectives

When you have studied this chapter you should be able to
understand:
1 the nature of fixed and variable costs;
2 the limits to specialisation, especially the size of the
market;
3 why average costs fall and then rise, as output rises;
4 why large and small firms can co-exist, although not
necessarily in the same market;
5 the importance of market share;
6 some of the strategies open to business people;
7 how economists classify the structures of different
industries.

2 Introduction

'Combien?' 'Was kostet?' are words we soon learn when we go to
French- and German-speaking countries, because costs are important. In this chapter we shall examine how costs vary with
output, and see how some firms are large and others small. We
shall see how people and areas specialise and the drawbacks
associated with such specialisation. We shall briefly examine
some theoretical structures of industries, ranging from thousands of firms to a single monopoly, noting how price and output
are determined. It is a part of economics where you can learn as
a team, sharing your knowledge with each other. Note that
economists use 'firm' to mean company, sole trader and nationalised industry, as well as the banker's narrow meaning of partner-
ship. Confusing, isn't it?

3 Costs

Economists use the term *cost* in what seem to be two senses, but, on closer examination, they are two ways of looking at the same principle. First, they often use it just as the person-in-the-street does, to mean the outlays or expenditures undertaken in order to manufacture a product or provide a service. Second, they also regard cost as what is termed *opportunity cost* – the opportunity to produce something else which is given up when we produce a particular commodity. One example is the lack of motorway service areas on the M25, because the authorities would not sacrifice the crops which could be produced from the land on which the areas would have been built.

However, there is no real conflict between the two concepts because the money value of the expenditures or outlays is merely the result of bidding against people who have alternative uses for the factors of production purchased. If steel can be used to make both cars and lawn-mowers, then the lawn-mower manufacturers must pay at least the same price for their steel as the motor car manufacturers would pay.

3.1 Fixed and variable costs

Some costs are fixed: they change only when the firm begins or ceases production. The premises of a bank branch are a reasonable example – not the best, because premises can be extended and rents may rise every five or seven years. The important point, however, is that as output increases, so there are more units to bear these *overheads* as they are sometimes called.

Other costs vary directly with output: labour and materials are obvious examples. A branch bank takes on more business, so its staff numbers rise, along with costs of postage, telephones, etc. But in banking the greatest variable cost is the *cost of funds*: if more deposits are needed then they must be bid for, either by paying interest or providing better current account services.

3.2 Marginal and average costs

Here the business person and the economist part company again, having been in agreement over fixed and variable costs, because the economist uses marginal in the sense of 'extra', or 'incremental' or 'additional' and most business people do not.

They usually use it to denote the difference or 'mark-up' between cost and selling price, their *profit margin*.

If we add all the marginal costs for the first ten units of output and divide by ten, we get the average cost of these ten units. Now, if the marginal cost of the eleventh unit is *above* the average cost of the ten, the new average cost of the eleven units will also be higher than for ten units. Try it on a piece of paper: average cost of ten units is 12p (total cost 10 × 12p = 120p); the marginal cost of the eleventh is 15p (total cost 120 + 15 = 135; divide by 11 and the new average cost is...).

So, to get average costs down we must keep marginal costs down, or, possibly, pare the fixed costs, e.g. move to cheaper premises or try to negotiate a lower rent.

4 Specialisation

Specialisation is found in many aspects of social life: in clubs and societies to catering for our hobbies, in many team sports – football, cricket and hockey – and in business. Not all shops sell everything, not all factories make everything. Even banks and insurance companies specialise to a certain extent. For instance, Hambro's is a merchant bank with extensive Scandinavian connections, while Lloyds Bank has wide-ranging operations in South America. Building societies are an example of specialised financial institutions which, since the Building Societies Act 1986, are trying to sell a wider range of products.

Economists often refer to Robinson Crusoe because for him specialisation was virtually impossible. A single person on a desert island has to do everything. As the population gets bigger, so specialists can develop. Thus, many hamlets do not even have a shop; if they grow large enough to be a village then they may have a shop and post office. Larger villages may have a full-time vicar, doctor and a primary school, although the secondary school children will still be 'bussed' to school several miles away, in the nearest town. Here there should be at least one bank, a fire station and a health centre, as well as a wide range of shops. Each of these – banks, shops and public services – will regard the population of the town and the surrounding villages and hamlets as comprising its 'market', i.e. its customers. The larger the market, the greater the amount of specialisation possible. In this country, London is the classic example, with a population large enough to support three universities

(London, City and Brunel), eight polytechnics and several large teaching hospitals, to give examples from just education and medicine.

4.1 Division of labour

In Chapter 1 we touched upon the factors of production – land, labour and capital – and here we will show how they too can become specialised. Land is capable of supporting only one activity at a time, e.g. grassland for animals, cultivated land for crops, land for housing or shops or factories. Capital, which we will define as machinery and buildings, is similar. A bulldozer cannot harvest grain and offices cannot easily be converted into factories.

But labour is different. We are flexible and can be trained to do a number of different tasks, although re-training is harder as we grow older. It was Adam Smith, known as the 'father of economics' who first set out the principles of the division of labour over 200 years ago. He took the example of pin-making, identifying eighteen different processes on which workers could specialise. Instead of a worker making perhaps ten pins a day if he or she did everything, if eighteen workers each specialised in one process then their average output could rise to 4800 a day – a 480-fold increase in productivity. In other words, marginal and average costs have both fallen dramatically.

The modern-day counterpart to the soul-destroying pin manufacture is perhaps the assembly line of a motor car factory; the 'track' as it is known. Here, each worker used to be responsible for perhaps only four or five nuts but, recently, robots have begun to do the work instead of humans.

Obviously, to use such processes in manufacturing requires a large number of customers: it is the volume car manufacturers, such as Austin Rover, Ford and Vauxhall, which use robotics rather than Lotus and other manufacturers of custom-built cars. In other words, the *division of labour*, which is that part of specialisation applying to workers, *is limited by the extent of the market*, just as with all forms of specialisation.

Earlier in this chapter we mentioned that banks can specialise, so what about the division of labour in banking? Does the principle still apply? The answer is, as you will realise, 'yes', but it is limited by the size of the market, which means the size of your branch because the larger the market the larger the branch. In a small village sub-branch open once a week, the cashier will do many things: taking orders for foreign currency, travellers cheques, statement requests, cheque books. These are enquiries which would be handled by the foreign clerk or one of the enquiries clerks at the main branch. To have a full-time foreign clerk a branch might need to have a staff of, say, twenty, but even he/she might not be expected to handle documentary credits. These might be opened or advised by the regional overseas branch, up to 100 miles away perhaps and serving over 100 main banking branches.

4.2 Internal economies of scale

Economies of scale is economic jargon for *lower average costs of production on a large scale.* Specialisation enables considerable reductions in costs to be achieved. Labour can become highly trained; specialised machinery can be employed; management can be divided into finance, production and sales; advertising can be employed to increase sales still further; better terms can be negotiated for credit from banks and suppliers.

All these 'economies' are achievable *within* the firm, as it grows bigger.

4.3 External economies of scale

These economies arise as the industry grows bigger, i.e. *outside* the firm. For instance, a trade paper may begin publication to give more up-to-date information to firms in the industry. Software houses may begin to write computer programs for the industry. Sub-contractors may develop, as with contract harvesting for farmers, and farm secretarial agencies.

Specialist firms may be founded to help the industry. In London for example, there are one or two specialists who advise foreign banks on some of the problems in setting up a London branch or representative office. Sometimes, the industry has become localised – as with cotton textiles in Lancashire and wool in Yorkshire. This facilitates further specialisation within groups of towns and enables technical colleges to help to train the employees. Apart from London, examples of such external economies in the financial services industry are the courses for the Credit Card Certificate provided at Northampton, Southend and Brighton, where there are large numbers of employees of Barclaycard, Access and Trustcard respectively.

4.4 Diseconomies

Costs do not continue to fall, mainly because the management problems become much more difficult as the firm becomes larger. Bureaucracy may stifle initiative in the drive to ensure the co-ordination of the various parts of the firm. Also, the original factory may be incapable of being expanded, so that it is cheaper to relocate to a new site and close down the old one rather than to run two factories simultaneously.

4.5 Integration

Sometimes firms expand not by establishing new operations but by purchasing firms in the same industry – their local rivals perhaps or, more frequently, those operating some distance away. Economists term this expansion *horizontal integration*. It nearly always involves purchases of other firms operating at the same stage of the production or distribution process.

  Vertical integration is another form of expansion. It involves a firm beginning to operate at a different stage of the industry. A steel manufactory, for instance, may buy a coal mine; the Milk Marketing Board owns Dairycrest, which supplies milk to shops. The Kuwait Petroleum Company has begun to purchase filling stations in the UK, which operate under the name Q8! Vertical integration does not necessarily have to involve a purchase but buying an existing operation is quicker than trying to set up a new one. The Abbey National Building Society's vertical integration into estate agencies will be largely by franchising. It will provide products, training and uniforms for the agencies, which it will not own. In banking we have seen horizontal integration when two banks merge; as when the Royal Bank of Scotland merged with Williams and Glyn's in the early 1980s; vertical integration is exemplified by banks buying estate agencies (which introduce new customers for loans) and, in advance of the Big Bang, buying firms of stockbrokers.

4.6 Location of industry

As we saw earlier, some localities become very specialised: textiles are a classic example, not only in Lancashire and Yorkshire but in Nottingham, Leicester, Macclesfield, Belfast and Dundee. More recent examples of 'high-tech' areas with large numbers of computer and bio-chemical firms are the

M3–M4 corridor from Heathrow to Reading and Basingstoke and the area around Cambridge.

But areas can become over-dependent on a particular industry which, if it begins to decline, will cause acute problems. Chatham was very dependent on its naval dockyard until it closed in 1984 and it has taken a great deal of effort to establish new enterprises there to provide employment for former dockyard workers.

In general, there are two main forces determining the location of industry: the pull of *resources* (mining is a classic example) and the pull of the *market* (brewing is a popular example). Obviously, mines must be where the minerals are and beer, because it is bulky, is expensive to transport. Hence, many local breweries still exist, even in these days of bulk tankers and brewing under licence from another brewer.

Banking is an example of the pull of the market; London is the big one, here. You may ask: isn't it also the pull of all the bank clerks in London? The answer is that a trained labour force does help but then, to clinch the point, look at Jersey. Here, the market which is a tax haven is so strong that the banks have to *import* labour from the mainland. Labour shortages, as in London and Jersey, demonstrate the pull of the market because banks set up there in spite of the difficulties of recruitment.

5 Perfect competition

Economists have an array of theoretical models of firms and industries, ranging from *monopoly*, with one firm in the industry, to *perfect competition*, where there are thousands of firms, none of which is able to influence the market price in any way whatsoever.

Perfect competition theory rests on the following assumptions:

1 Every firm in the industry is so small that it cannot influence the market price; the effect is to make every firm a price-taker rather than a price-maker.
2 Firms are free to enter and leave the industry if they so wish; the result is that supply becomes fairly elastic.
3 Factors of production are also mobile, thus adding to the elastic nature of the supply curve.
4 There are no transport costs, i.e. no local monopolies and no differences in price due to distance from the factories.

5 There is no ignorance in the market as to prices, so that all buyers buy only at the market price.

Now we come to the crux of the theory. If each firm accepts the market price and cannot affect it by its own actions then each firm must be able to sell as much of its output as it wishes at that constant market price. In economist's language, its demand curve is infinitely elastic, being flat and parallel with the horizontal scale, while marginal revenue equals price.

But this doesn't mean that each firm can sell at a profit as many goods as it can produce, because the theory has no special assumptions about the cost structures of firms. Traditional economics tells us that each firm will expand output until marginal cost equals marginal revenue. Now, marginal revenue is fixed and equal to price, so marginal cost becomes crucial as the sole determinant of each firm's level of output.

Notice, too, that the theory does not say that all firms in the industry are of the *same* size – only that all are so small that none can influence the price. As we saw in Section 3, marginal costs will eventually rise so the key to profitability is cost. Assuming that the output is of sufficiently high quality to be sold, costs will determine profits.

In Section 4 we introduced economies of scale. Where do they fit into the theory of perfect competition? The answer is they don't! Under perfect competition the firms are very small, so that economies of scale have only a minimal effect on costs and hence on permitting the expansion of firms.

5.1 Perfect competition – in practice

If you bear in mind the importance of costs in determining profitability under perfect competition, together with the virtual absence of economies of scale, you will be able to see the relevance of the concept in helping us to understand practical examples. To some extent, and only some extent, farming is a fair example of perfect competition, because most farms are so small that their output cannot have any effect on price. Dairy farmers are a classic example. Under the EEC's former dairy price regulations dairy farmers could sell all the milk they could at a fixed price, determined every year by the EEC.

The UK Ministry of Agriculture used to give advice to dairy farmers as to how to increase output and reduce costs. However, the EEC is now imposing quotas or limits on milk production, and countries and their farmers which produce more than their quota have to pay a fine, called a *levy*.

Suddenly, that wonderful elastic demand curve has begun to slope downwards very dangerously.

Also, when we look at the other assumptions we see that in many ways farming is not really a good example of perfect competition. First, it is not easy to become a farmer – lengthy training comes first and farms are still very expensive to buy. Movement in the industry is one way – outward, as farm workers leave and more land is used for other uses such as roads and housing. So factor mobility is limited. Also land is not very mobile – you can't grow cereals on hill farms.

Second, there is a lack of information readily available so that farmers have to rely on advisory services provided by fertiliser manufacturers and the Ministry of Agriculture. However, costs are still very important, given the fixed prices reviewed every year.

Now, let us turn to a market where banks play an important role – the foreign exchange market in the world's leading currencies, such as the US dollar, the Deutschemark and the Japanese yen. Massive as some of the world's largest commercial banks are, it is still difficult to imagine that any one of them could alter the exchange rate by its own purchases and sales of that particular currency. Yet, the market is not perfect in the economist's sense because central banks – which act to protect their economies and their currencies – frequently intervene in the market for the very purpose of altering the rate. This 'foreign exchange management' obviously precludes the existence of perfect competition.

To take a second banking example, the London discount market is not a perfect market because the Bank of England acts as lender of last resort, usually to influence the interest rates, as we shall see in Chapter 10.

6 Market share

Under perfect competition, producers are not really interested in finding out their share of the market, it is an irrelevant fact. Much more important is the need to reduce cost.

However, once we leave perfect competition and move to markets where the suppliers can influence the price of their product (and other suppliers' prices) by their own actions then market shares become increasingly important. Competition among the few can involve intense struggles to capture a larger percentage of total market sales. Yet, when we reach the other end of the spectrum from perfect competition – monopoly – we find that market share is of little interest, because the monopolist has 100% of the market.

Outside these two limiting cases – perfect competition and monopoly – suppliers are faced with downward sloping average revenue (demand) curves and somewhat steeper marginal revenue curves. Not only do they have to watch their costs but they must also make decisions about prices as well.

But let us get back to market share, because we need to do a few percentages. At the beginning of Big Bang in October 1986, there were 28 *market makers* (combined brokers and jobbers) in the gilt-edged market. On average, the market share of each would be $\frac{1}{28} \times 100 = 3.6\%$. However, some were much bigger and well established than others and were probably aiming at a market share of 10%. This would depress the average of the market share available to the others (some 25), so that they could expect to have perhaps no more than 3% of the market.

When we get to retail banking (High Street banking), petrol stations, breakfast cereals and volume car production, we are dealing not with 25 or 30 suppliers but with perhaps six or seven. Consequently market shares are that much larger, with perhaps an average in the region of 15–17%.

6.1 Concentration ratios

Economists have a way of measuring the degree of *concentration* in an industry, by ascertaining the combined market shares of the leading firms in that industry. The ratios can be calculated for the three leading firms, or for the top five, or for any number. The 'five firm concentration ratio' for the gilt-edged market makers might be (and it's a pure guess) 35%, but for retail banking it could be 70%, i.e. the total market shares of the Big 4 clearers and Royal Bank of Scotland. For an industry like cement making the 'two firm concentration ratio' could approach 80%.

Under the Fair Trading Act 1973, the critical market share is 25% controlled by a single firm. Such firms can be investigated by the Monopolies and Mergers Commission (*see* Section 8.2).

6.2 Market strategies

As firms get bigger, therefore, they become increasingly concerned about their market share. Some firms will make a conscious decision to maintain their market share or even to increase it wherever possible. Other firms may not wish to be so aggressive, preferring to maximise their profits. Others may strive to become a market leader, e.g. in design, technology or in price setting. They wish to be the firm to which their competitors look for guidance. Many would say that Barclays Bank strove for many years to be the market leader: first with a credit card, first with students' gift schemes, a leader with cash dispensers in the late 1960s and, in the 1970s, frequently the first to change its base rate, the price of its main product – loans.

You may say that this suggests that firms do not pursue profits all the time. To a certain extent this is true, because firms must always consider future profits as well as current profits. For instance, if a firm does not invest in research now for future products it may find its market share falling and so face a reduction in future profits. Extra profits today, achieved by cutting back on research, may cause profits to fall in, say, five years' time. It therefore has to decide which is more worthwhile – £1m of profits today or more than £1m in five years' time.

7 Oligopoly

Oligopoly is a term derived from the same Greek word as *oligarchy*. It refers to competition among the few, in industries where there are perhaps five or six major suppliers. Retail petrol distribution is a classic example, with seven major companies – Shell, BP, Exxon (Esso), Mobil, Texaco, Socal (Chevron in the UK) and Gulf. There are also minor companies, such as Bulldog, ICI which is found only in NE England, and Q8, to name but a few.

Oligopoly is remembered by students chiefly for its *kinked demand curve*, as will be seen in the diagrams in economics textbooks. In other words, no oligopolist can raise prices independently because this would lose all the customers, so oligopoly has a relatively flat demand (average revenue) curve for price *increases*. Worse, however, is the effect of a price *fall*, because this would attract so many customers from the rivals that their market shares would fall. To protect their market shares they would reduce their prices to the same extent as our oligopolist did, so that the final result is not much different than before the fall was precipitated. The oligopolists are thus faced with a steep demand curve for price *decreases*. The kink in the demand curve occurs at the prevailing price, where it changes from a gentle slope to a steep slope.

Our oligopolist still increases output to a point where marginal revenue equals marginal cost. The unique feature is that the cost structure is such that economies of scale mean that marginal cost equals marginal revenue at such a high level of output that it comprises perhaps 15 per cent of the total market.

7.1 Oligopoly – in practice

The peculiar shape of the demand curve entails oligopolists being 'locked in' to the current price. They have to move in concert with their rivals if their market shares are to remain intact and their cost structures protected – we must remember that the industry's economies of scale are such that the oligopolists need to operate at about 15 per cent of total industry production in order for marginal cost to equal marginal revenue.

So, how do oligopolists compete? The answer is in many ways except price. Examples are:

(a) location. Petrol filling stations and High Street banks cluster along the main roads.
(b) heavy expenditure on advertising, designed to increase brand loyalties among customers.
(c) emphasising quality or uniqueness. Nat West are 'the Action Bank', the Midland are 'the Listening Bank', while Lloyds claims to be 'a thoroughbred amongst banks'.
(d) gift promotions. Many of us have good collections of mugs and wine glasses from our usual petrol station. Gifts are also now featuring in banks' marketing tactics.

As well as petrol and oil, and retail (High Street) banking, brewing is now another oligopolistic industry and is the subject of a Monopolies and Mergers Commission report due to be published in 1988.

8 Monopoly

The monopolist enjoys, if that is the right word, being the sole producer of a commodity or a service. British Telecom used to be a monopoly supplier of telephone and telex services, with the exception of Hull. Now it has competition on inland and international lines from Mercury plc. The Post Office used to have a monopoly of all mail: now it faces competition from courier companies on international services and in large towns.

Monopolists have to make a crucial decision in pricing and output policy. They can control one but not the other. Which is it to be? If they force up the price they may frighten away too many customers so that they cannot take full advantage of the usually large economies of scale. If they aim to sell all that they can produce, the price may be too low.

Monopolists follow the same great rule that other producers do and equate marginal cost and marginal revenue. However, they are unique in that marginal cost and revenue are inter-dependent. If they change output then they must change price in order to be able to sell the output. You must remember that they cannot force everybody to buy their product. There is nothing in the theory which says that monopolies enjoy a completely inelastic demand. Their demand is certainly inelastic but most consumers will be deterred from buying the same quantity of their product if they raise their price.

Nevertheless, monopolists do try and group their customers to see if the demand curves (and hence marginal revenues) differ. For instance, public utilities such as gas, electricity, water and telecommunications charge differently if the consumer is running a business. The rental of a telephone line costs more for a commercial user than it does for a private person. A better example of this *price discrimination* comes, surprisingly, from the entertainment industry. Theatres charge a wide range of prices according to where the customer sits. Another example is at a Spanish bull ring, where spectators pay more for seats in the shade than seats in the sun – yet the cost of building and servicing the seats is the same. A third example, partly of discrimination but also of product development, is soccer, where you can stand on the terraces to watch the same match as seen by the business people wining and dining in their executive suites. Obviously, it costs more to provide an executive suite than it does to provide standing room on the terraces, but the marginal revenues are very different.

One danger monopolists have to watch for is the possibility that by maximising short-term profit they will cause another firm to enter the market and try to share some of the profit. If this is likely, they will not raise prices to the point where MC = MR and profits are maximised but will limit them below that level. This *limit pricing* will reduce profits now but should ensure that they continue at that level for some time to come. It is another example of the need to take a longer view than maximising today's profits, similar to the need for research expenditure which we saw earlier.

8.1 Monopoly – in practice

As you probably realise, pure or 100% monopoly is as rare as perfect competition, but there is always the possibility (probability might be a better way of describing it) that suppliers will come together to fix prices or output. The economist's term for such an agreement is *cartel*, derived from the German 'das Kartell' because of the development of the practice by German chemical companies. The American word is *trust*.

Perhaps the most notorious recent cartel is the Organisation of the Petroleum Exporting Countries (OPEC) which raised the price of crude oil dramatically in 1973 and again in 1979/80. Since then, however, other producers such as Mexico and the UK have undercut OPEC while Russian exports of natural gas have begun to provide further competition for OPEC crude in Western Europe. Consequently, OPEC has gone on the defensive and begun to limit output rather than control price. Remember, as a monopolist it can't do both. By fixing output, which can be monitored more easily than prices, the cartel hopes to discourage price-cutting by its members.

Cartels used to be found in banking and finance. Until 1971, the London clearing banks had an interest rate structure related to the Bank Rate announced weekly by the Bank of England. Whenever Bank Rate changed, the clearing banks' interest rate structures moved in unison, for both advances and deposits. As part of the wide-ranging changes known as Competition and Credit Control, this practice ceased and each bank has since announced its own interest rate structures, usually linked to its base rate, upon which rates for many of its loans and advances are calculated.

Until recently, building societies followed a somewhat similar practice, following the Building Societies Association's recommended rates for deposits/shares and home loans.

Cartels were not known as such in Adam Smith's time but he was fully aware that business people seldom meet together without conspiring to raise prices. Indeed, the medieval guilds were, in effect, cartels. Certainly, meetings do provide the opportunity for tacit (hidden) rather than open collusion.

Tacit collusion often takes the form of price leadership. Usually this is *dominant-firm* leadership, as with Barclays Bank in the 1970s, when it competed with National Westminster to be the first to announce a change in base rate. Other banks frequently became passive and merely followed Barclays to protect their market shares.

Sometimes, however, the price leadership comes from a smaller aggressive firm. Thus, Williams and Glyn's, before it became merged with the Royal Bank of Scotland, led the way in price-cutting as interest rates rose in the 1970s. It also seems that some of the independent petrol companies (such as Jet) led the majors in trying to curtail price increases when crude oil prices rose in line with OPEC policy, so that pump prices were not as high as the majors would have wished. Such price leadership is termed *barometric*.

8.2 Monopoly – government intervention

In the face of the potential power of monopolists to restrict output and so raise prices, it is not surprising that governments in many countries regulate monopolies. In the USA, the policy began almost a century ago and was known as *trust-busting*. The EEC, too, has its regulations, under a number of articles of the Treaty of Rome, but these apply only to trade between member states.

The UK has two important pieces of legislation: the Monopolies and Mergers Act 1965 and the Fair Trading Act 1973. The latter created the post of Director-General of Fair Trading, whose office can refer monopolies and proposed mergers to the Monopolies and Mergers Commission for close examination. The guideline as to a monopoly situation is if 25% of the market is controlled by a single seller or buyer. The latter case is known as *monopsony*. It could apply in cases such as the pay of civil servants, where there is only one purchaser of the labour in question but, not surprisingly, the Commission's work does not extend to the labour market. Prior to 1973, the critical level of market share was 33%.

Once an industry or proposed merger has been referred to it by the Director-General of Fair Trading, the Monopolies and Mergers Commission will prepare a report. The Secretary of State for Trade and Industry has the final say as to whether a merger should be permitted or whether a monopoly situation should continue. In the summer of 1987, great publicity was given to the proposed take-over of British Caledonian by British Airways. The bid was referred to the Commission, with a request for a speedy report.

There are other controls. Under the Companies Acts, any company which owns more than 5% of another company's ordinary share capital must declare its interest. Moreover, the Take-Over Code of the Stock Exchange requires a company with more than 29.9% of another's ordinary share capital to make an offer to buy the remaining 70.1%. This offer could result in the Director-General of Fair Trading referring it to the Commission.

In banking and finance the Bank of England exercises a watching brief. It is believed that the Bank was relieved that the proposed merger of the Royal Bank of Scotland with the Hong Kong & Shanghai Banking Corporation was not allowed to proceed. Another banking merger which went to the Monopolies Commission (as it then was) was that of Barclays, Lloyds and Martins Banks in 1968. The Commission reported that the three-bank merger should be disallowed and that only the take-over of Martins by one of the other two should be permitted. In the event, Barclays bought Martins.

Two proposals which did not go to the Commission were the unsuccessful Lloyds Bank bid for Standard Chartered Bank in 1986 and the sale in 1987 by Midland Bank of its Scottish and Irish subsidiaries to the National Bank of Australasia.

Summary

Specialisation and economies of scale are very important, not only for workers involved, but also for their employers, because they enable firms to grow much larger. They are determined by technical and marketing influences but have been limited by managerial problems. However, the growth of PCs (personal computers) and telecommunications could mean a new future for small businesses.

Market shares are often a crucial goal for firms, with governments poised to investigate if one firm has more than (say) 25% or 33% of the market. Other important policies include price leadership, especially with oligopolies where six or seven firms usually change price together.

As bank employees your future working life could be determined by (a) specialisation, (b) the further rise of computers and (c) mergers and take-overs.

Questions

Some of the questions will enable the class to work together as a group and show you how groups do or do not function successfully. It may show natural leaders arising: if not, then the lecturer should nominate tasks or the group elect a leader. You may be involved in supervisory skills in economics!

Care: In seeking answers to these questions, many of which can be tackled jointly by a class working together, you should never use information which may be available to you from your bank work. The latter is strictly confidential.

1 List the various estate agencies in the area where you live. From the numbers of boards outside houses and flats, estimate the market share of each agency.

2 Telephone the agencies and ask for details of their commission charges (to avoid annoyance, each member of a class can contact a different agency). If the fees are very similar, use the data in Question 1 to determine whether the market is oligopolistic or monopolistic. If the fees vary, discuss among yourselves why some agencies charge more than others (newcomers may charge less).

3 Does one agency tend to be 'market leader', e.g. first to open on Sundays or first to use colour photographs?

4 During your studies, monitor these agencies for: (a) amalgamations; (b) purchases by banks, building societies or insurance companies; (c) new entrants.

5 Which firm or industry is the largest employer in the area where you live? How large is the largest firm in your area? How much specialisation is possible, e.g. does it have its own motor transport department, staff canteen or sports and social club?

6 How large is the largest local branch of a retail bank? Does it have more than 50 employees?

7 How many firms deliver milk to homes in your area? Why is the minimum price of fresh milk still fixed by the government?

8 What are the fixed costs faced by:
  (a) banks?
  (b) building societies?
  (c) estate agencies?

9 If the European Community produces too much food, why does it not lower the prices it pays to farmers for their output? (*Note*: farmers have votes.)

10 List as many 'one-person businesses' as you can. Why are so many builders, farmers, shopkeepers and restaurateurs one-person businesses? Are there many one-person businesses actually manufacturing goods? If not, why not?

11 Repeat Questions 1–3 for (a) local petrol filling stations; (b) supermarkets; (c) retail banks.

12 How many local filling stations are also becoming 'convenience stores'? What other goods do they now sell?

13 Assess the amount of specialised work available in a seven-person branch of a bank and contrast it with the specialisation possible in a branch with a staff of 70.

14 Compare and contrast the filling stations of major oil companies with those of a small independent company in terms of: price, amenities (toilets, etc.), availability of other goods.

15 To what extent might there be considerable economies of scale in the manufacture of Rolls Royce cars?

16 'Economies of scale mean that perfect competition is impossible.' Explain.

17 If a clearing bank were to bid for a building society, which will be possible when some societies become public limited liability companies, do you think that the proposed bid should be investigated by the Monopolies and Mergers Commission?

18 If a Japanese bank were to bid for a UK clearing bank or a building society, should the proposed bid be permitted by the government?

19 Do you think that the continued development of small personal computers and the rise of small firms, e.g. very small real-ale breweries, could indicate that the age of the large firm might be ended next century?

20 What are the economies of scale in a retail banking network of 1500 branches?

4
Prices and output – the nation

1 Objectives

When you have studied this chapter, you should be aware of how the general levels of prices and of output are determined for the whole economy and not just for a particular firm or industry. You should:

1 appreciate the problem of inflation;

2 appreciate the problem of unemployment;

3 be aware of how governments try to resolve these two major problems of industrialised countries;

4 be aware that inflation and unemployment often cannot be reduced together;

5 appreciate the problem of the business cycle;

6 have a knowledge of some of the many ways in which governments can influence economies.

2 Introduction

So far in this book, we have studied the prices of particular goods and services. Now we are going to examine the general level of all prices in the economy. Your own experience will probably tell you that the trend of the prices of most goods and services is upwards. In fact, it has been so continually throughout history, with some exceptions; prices have risen every year since 1935, so that most people cannot remember the falling prices of the 1920s and early 1930s. Sometimes prices rise rapidly, as in 1975 and 1980; in the summer of 1987 they were rising at about 4–4.5% a year.

Although prices have been rising for over 50 years, there is a brighter side to the picture. Output, including that of services as well as goods, has also been rising for most of this time, and the actual falls in output seen widely in the inter-war period are now part of history. In general, output is on a rising trend although certain industries such as ship building are still declining.

In order to curb inflation and reduce unemployment, governments of all political persuasions now intervene much more in an economy than they did and we will begin to look at some of the ways they try to do this. Later in the book we will go into greater detail, to see how banks are affected.

3 The general level of prices

There are two aspects of the general level of prices in a country, i.e. how the inhabitants are affected and how foreigners are affected. After all, they buy from and sell to us, so we must consider them – which we do in Chapter 9. However, for this chapter we consider what is termed the *internal purchasing power of money*.

Arithmetically, if prices in general rise then money's purchasing power falls. If prices double then we say that the purchasing power of money has halved: if £1 buys now what 50p bought ten years ago then £1 now is worth what 50p was – and 50p is half of £1.

You may (or rather must) ask: how do we know exactly how much prices have risen? The answer is that it is difficult but we will go into some detail about this in the next section. Here we must state that we need a very wide-ranging measure, to cover all the various transactions which go into producing goods and services. But to get a wide measure takes time and we need to measure money's purchasing power fairly frequently. Moreover, we do not want to be plagued by revisions of the figures as frequently occurs with many economic statistics. So, we have come to rely mainly on one particular set of statistics, called the General Index of Retail Prices (RPI), which is published monthly, on a Friday in the middle of the month. These prices are retail; there are separate statistics for producers' input prices and their output prices, as well as estimates for the whole economy (called the *deflator*).

Prices of financial assets – currencies, houses, stocks and shares – are excluded.

3.1 How the price level is measured (the RPI)

Rather like somebody doing their shopping, the economist looks at a very long list of goods and services bought by most people. Each item is recorded and compared with its price at the *base date*, which is January 1987.

But not all items are of equal importance to people in their spending habits. Salt, as we saw in Chapter 2, forms only a small part of our monthly expenditure, whereas meat (red and white) is more important. Accordingly, the government asks a group of households, spread around the country and covering most income levels except the very rich and the very poor to record their expenditure over a period.

From these records, the statisticians are able to calculate the importance (the *weighting* as it is called) of each item. The weights are then calculated so they all add to 1000.

The prices are collected – on a Tuesday to avoid price fluctuations at the beginning or end of a week – by a team of clerks who visit the shops and hairdressing salons, etc. Then the prices are compared with those of January 1987 and expressed as a ratio of that date's price. Suppose that the item is a 275 ml can of light ale, costing 35p now compared with 31p in January 1987. The price has risen by $\frac{35}{31} = 1.29$.

Now we need to know the weighting of this item – suppose it is 7 (out of 1000). We then multiply it by 7 to get 9.03 which is added to all the other price increases which have been multiplied by their weightings. For the sake of simplicity we will take a chicken and then call everything else 'other'. Table 4.1 shows how the RPI is calculated.

Table 4.1

Item	Price Jan 87 (1)	Price now (2)	Change (3)	Weighting (4)	(3) × (4)
Light ale	31p	35p	1.29	7	9.03
Chicken	£1.47	£1.58	1.07	11	11.77
Other	£103	£108	1.05	982	1031.10
RPI				1000	1051.90

The index for the month in question is published to three whole numbers and rounded to one decimal place. The last column 1051.90 then becomes 105.19, which is then rounded to 105.2 (compared to 100.0 in January 1987). Since then, prices have risen by 5.2%, so beer drinkers are unlucky with their light ale prices! (29% rise). Perhaps the government has raised the duty (tax) on beer.

As we have mentioned, the index is never revised because the figures have been used in sensitive wage negotiations for many years and now they are used in capital gains tax calculations and what is called *current cost accounting*. The index's old name was *cost of living index*, giving us an idea of what it tried to measure – how much it cost a family to live.

It is also used to calculate the value of index-linked National Savings Certificates and state retirement pensions. The latter are raised each April in line with the annual rise in the index to the preceding September. That list of how the government uses it officially does not include all the negotiations in which it is used to support or reject various proposals, e.g. a wage claim or offer, or a proposal to raise telephone charges. Many household insurance policies link the value of the house's contents to the index.

3.2 How government can directly influence the RPI

To get back to our can of beer – or rather the tax on it. Governments can influence the index by changing taxes and subsidies on goods and services; a notorious example occurred in 1974 when the standard rate of VAT was lowered from 10% to 8% just before the second general election of that year. In 1979, just after winning the next election, the Conservatives raised VAT from 8% to 15%, jerking up the index by some 3 or 4% in one or two months as the VAT increases were passed on to the goods in the shops.

Sometimes the index is used as part of the calculations to measure real wages (real means something ignoring changes in the value of money). If wages have risen by 9% since January 1987 but prices generally have risen by only 5.2% then real wages (i.e. their purchasing power) have increased by 3.6% ($\frac{109 \cdot 0}{105 \cdot 2} \times 100$).

But our gross wages bear a large number of deductions before our bank accounts are credited with the net pay, and income tax and national insurance contributions are the largest deductions as a rule.

The government can alter the purchasing power of wages in several direct ways:

(a) by taxes on goods – e.g. VAT, petrol, cigarettes and alcohol;
(b) by subsidies – rare in industrialised countries but common in countries such as Egypt which subsidise petrol and food;
(c) by rationing and price controls – common in wartime;
(d) by changes in income tax, so that take-home pay changes as well. Many of us hope that the basic rate will be reduced to 25p soon, because our net income will rise. Others fear a reduction in public spending to allow the cuts to be made.
(e) by changes in national insurance contributions, which bear quite heavily on those earning up to about £12 000 a year.

The UK government has thus devised a further index to show how price rises have been offset or aggravated by changes in income tax and national insurance contributions (changes in taxes on goods and services will, of course, be reflected in the Retail Prices Index). Not surprisingly, the new index is called the Tax and Price Index (TPI). It began very shortly after the Conservative Party came to power in 1979, but, as the rate of inflation has fallen faster than the taxes included, it has not received much attention.

3.3 Types of inflation – speed

For some reason, description of rates of inflation is related to horses. When in low single figures, e.g. 3–5% pa, it is described as *creeping*. When the inflation rate rises to (say) 25% or 40% pa the adjective becomes *trotting*; when 100% a year or more, inflation becomes *galloping*.

Some countries, such as West Germany and Switzerland, have for years had relatively low inflation rates. Others such as Israel and many Latin American countries have had galloping inflation for several years, although after 1985 Israel reduced its inflation rate to the low 'teens.

Occasionally, there are outbreaks of hyper-inflation, as in Germany in 1922–3 (not the 1930s as many students state) and briefly after the second world war. In hyper-inflation prices change *daily*, so that wages are paid daily: it leaves bitter memories as people's savings in cash and bank accounts lose all their value. Understandably, public opinion in Germany favours very low inflation.

3.4 Types of inflation – causes

As you might guess, there are two main causes: one acting through supply schedules and called *cost-push* inflation, and the other acting through demand schedules and called *demand-pull*. Since demand can pull prices up and since many prices form part of suppliers' costs, e.g. telephone calls, petrol and diesel, steel, it is very difficult to establish the prime cause. Certainly, if demand is weak (strictly elastic) then a rise in costs may have to be borne partly, if not largely, by the supplier, as we saw in Chapter 2.

Sometimes, governments can add to demand by their expenditure, as we shall see later. Sometimes, an external shock can cause extra inflationary pressure, as with the oil price rises of 1973 and 1979/80.

During the past 15 years the distinction between demand-pull and cost-push theories has become blurred, with demand-pull advocates emphasising the importance of the money supply and exchange rates. Opposed to this monetarist view of inflation are those who argue that inflation can be due to social reasons such as the actions of trade unions in seeking and achieving excessive wage increases or to outside influences such as a rise in import prices.

3.5 Effects of inflation

If *all* prices, including those in contracts e.g. rents, pensions, etc., fixed years ago were to change simultaneously there would be few problems associated with inflation. But they don't and that is the nub of the matter.

It used to be argued that 'inflation hits the pensioner' but nowadays the state retirement pension is increased annually in line with the Retail Prices Index, while many private pensions have also been increased somewhat. Savings deposited in banks and building societies have not increased in value in line with inflation although some National Savings products have been *index-linked* to the RPI. The most well-known of these are the index-linked National Savings Certificates, given the nickname 'Granny Bonds' because they were restricted to retirement pensioners at first.

Interest rates can be affected by inflation, often rising in line with prices but remaining lower than inflation. In the mid-1980s, however, interest rates did not fall as fast as the rate of

ey were *higher* than inflation. Economists call the
adjusted for the rate of inflation the *real* rate of
.y call everything such as output, exchange rates,
.d for inflation 'real'!) and when it is positive (interest
ᵣ.   er than inflation) the effects on the profits of companies wᵢ.th substantial borrowing can be devastating. Savers,
on the other hand, benefit from a positive real rate of interest.

So far, we have ignored the international aspects of inflation
but we must mention here that if one country experiences a
substantially higher rate of inflation than others then it will
find it more difficult to sell its exports and that foreign goods
will be cheaper in terms of its own currency. Accordingly, it will
eventually have to devalue its currency against those of its
major trading partners, unless the exchange rate is already
floating, in which case it should move down automatically.

Because they too are in business, banks are affected by rising
costs, especially salary and other personnel costs. However, their
major cost (interest paid) and their major source of revenue
(interest charged) are influenced by the Treasury and the Bank
of England, who may be unwilling to allow the markets to push
interest rates too high.

4 Gross domestic product (gdp)

This is probably the most difficult concept for students to visual-
ise and then understand. After all, we've all seen (or think we've
seen) a gallon of petrol or a ton of coal but you can't go out and
see a gdp in every town in the country. It is the nation's *total
output of goods and services*. If it is high you'll see many new
cars, new motorways, clean pavements, new filling stations, new
schools, new hospitals, busy shops, offices and factories. But, if
you stumble on the pavement, your bicycle breaks a spoke on a
pothole and your grandparents are on a two-year waiting list for
their hip operations, the economist will say it is all a result of
gdp not being as high as in other countries where these misfor-
tunes do not occur.

The word *gross* is used to denote that it is calculated before we
allow for replacing our capital assets – our *depreciation charges*
as the accountants would say. The word *domestic* is used because
we are considering only that output produced in this country –
some of it is produced abroad by factors of production owned by
UK firms (such as BP, ICI and Barclays Bank) and then the

profits are remitted back to the UK. The government can influence only the domestic part of our output and has little influence over (say) ICI in countries such as the USA and Australia. Accordingly gdp is the statistic the government watches rather than gnp (gross national product) which includes such income from abroad.

4.1 How gdp is measured

Here we are concentrating on the *product* part of gdp. *It comprises all goods and services produced within the country.* The list is enormous and we use money as the measuring rod rather than gallons, tons, accounts opened or lorries, vans and lathes built.

The way in which the calculations are made is to use the circular flow of income – your sales are often somebody else's costs of production; your salary is part of your employer's costs and goes (rapidly) to buy goods and services from other people. So, we can add up all the *expenditure* on final sales (excluding sales to wholesalers and processors) or we can add up all the wages, salaries and other *incomes* (rents, profits, etc.) of the three factors of production, which we saw briefly in Chapter 1 to be labour, land and capital, or we can add up all the *net output* of every industry and service.

Income method
Here we add:

(a) income from employment (wages and salaries before tax);
(b) income from self-employment (from sole traders and partnerships);
(c) gross profits of companies and public corporations.

Let's take a short example of a firm importing boomerangs from Australia, varnishing them and selling them in Earls Court, a part of London where many Australians live. The 'product' is the varnished boomerang – because that's all they've done to it. We do not count the import of the weapons, only the cost of the labour which has gone into varnishing them and the profit earned by the owner of the company. We'll return to this example again.

One point must be stressed. We do not include transfer payments such as pensions, child benefit and other social security benefits. This is because they are not income for factors of production in return for their output but are given to people as of right. Similarly, interest on national debt and dividends from shares are excluded.

Expenditure method
Here we add:

(a) *consumers' expenditure* (consumption): what we individuals eat and drink and enjoy, e.g. books, holidays, examination fees (!);

(b) *government consumption*: e.g. uniforms of the army, lighting for schools and for government offices;

(c) investment expenditure (*gross domestic fixed capital formation*) by companies (factories for example), by individuals (new houses for example) and government (new schools and motorways). Notice that it is *new* goods, not second-hand ones, which are counted.

(d) *exports less imports*. After all, we produce the exports for foreigners to buy and it is our production that we are measuring, so we must include exports. But total expenditure in categories (a), (b) and (c) includes imports (which we did not produce), so we exclude them here. The figures include services as well as goods.

(e) *increase in stocks and work in progress*. We've produced the goods, so we ought to include them even though they are in a warehouse waiting to be sold.

To return to our boomerang importers. In this case we take the value of their sales (under (a) consumers' expenditure) and subtract the cost of the imported unvarnished boomerangs under (d) net exports.

Output method
Here we add the net output of each industry or service – such as agriculture, mining, manufacturing, construction, banking and insurance, etc.

The boomerang firm's output is measured in the same way as the expenditure method, but other industries might be selling to each other (e.g. sales of coal to generate electricity) and these need to be netted out.

Banks are involved not only in producing services which go into gdp, e.g. cheque clearing, trustee services, etc. but also because they can sell savings products to the people involved in the income calculations, you and me, sole traders and companies, and loan/finance products to finance the categories involved on the expenditure side. Personal loans, credit cards, home loans, leasing and factoring are some of these products. Building societies compete with banks for the income of the employed and self-employed and for home loans to finance new houses. Larger items of capital investment, such as the Channel Tunnel, have to seek finance from the stock market as well as from banks.

4.2 How the elements of gdp interact

We have seen how your expenditure will be part of somebody else's salary and their employer's profits (or loss) but what happens if you don't spend all your income? The ordinary answer is: don't worry, somebody else will be spending more than their income. The crux comes when people *in general* start to underspend: somebody has to overspend to keep the circular flow moving freely.

There is always overspending occurring, particularly by large companies investing in expensive new factories and machinery. To achieve a steady circular flow of spending/income in the system they need people who do not spend and *financial intermediaries*, such as banks, pension funds, insurance companies, to channel the funds from the underspenders to the overspenders.

Now, we ought to consider two links between categories on the expenditure side of gdp. The first is called the *accelerator*.

Imagine a fleet of ten ships, each with a life of ten years and with one ship being replaced every year. If, say, demand for the fleet's services rises by 10% one year, business will increase and the ship due to be replaced that year will not be sufficient to provide the service now required. Another ship will need to be ordered, so that for that particular year two ships will be ordered. Thus a 10% rise in the demand for the use of that fleet's ships has resulted in a 100% rise in the owner's demand for new ships – from one to two. Moreover, when trade declines again, there will be complete lack of demand for new ships so that a 10% fall in demand for shipping services could lead to a 100% fall in new construction, with the ship being scrapped that year not needing to be replaced, because nine ships are able to provide the reduced service. Such a contraction in demand is very serious, because workers will most likely be made redundant.

This accelerator effect on the demand for capital goods such as ships is one reason for the very sharp booms and slumps in these capital goods industries.

The second link, the *multiplier*, is the knock-on effect of expenditure as it goes through the circular flow of income (allowing for savings of course). Suppose that the government increases the Christmas bonus for pensioners from £10 to £20, and that there are 4m recipients. This means that £80m will be given to them and, because they are elderly and many not very wealthy, most of it will be spent (let us say £75m). We saw in the previous section that the £80m is a *transfer payment* and not counted in gdp but the £75m of expenditure will count towards the expenditure way of calculating gdp. The shopkeepers will spend the £75m partly on wages for their assistants but are likely to order new stocks to replace those sold to the pensioners. The new orders mean more gdp. This second round of expenditure could total between £70m and £75m. And so the surge goes on, but it gets smaller each time as some of the income generated by the initial burst of expenditure is saved or spent on imports.

A better example of the multiplier will be the Channel Tunnel, as the contractors receive their fees and spend them on wages, new plant and machinery. The unfinished Tunnel will count towards gdp because there is also a category of *changes in stocks* which we must consider. Stocks include work-in-progress on large construction contracts such as ships, airliners, etc. and increases in them must be included in gdp. On the other hand, decreases in stocks must be *subtracted* from gdp because the 'contra' to the expenditure is not the production of a replacement item but an empty place on a shelf in a warehouse.

If we have large leakages in the form of savings or imports the surge of expenditure may dwindle rapidly – £80m; £64m (£16m saved or spent on imports); £51.2m (£64m – £12.8m); £40.1m; £32.8m and so on. If the *marginal propensity to consume* is high then the tapering effect will be minimal, as in the earlier example where only £5m of the first £80m was lost.

5 The business cycle

Gdp does not grow or fall each year to the same extent; usually it grows but occasionally it falls and the important question is: by how much will it grow or fall?

In general, there is a pattern or cycle to the changes, in this order: a slump of low growth or even falls, then recovery with rising growth rates, then a boom with growth rates at their peak, followed by a recession of falling growths and returning to the slump conditions again.

The government's Central Statistical Office has calculated that the last peak in the business cycle occurred in May 1979 and the last trough in May 1981. With six years of relative growth behind us, and a five to seven year cycle, we must expect the next peak very soon, *very likely before this book is published.*

5.1 Why the cycle occurs

Economists are generally agreed as to why the cycle occurs, at least in theory, but they often disagree as to how the situation at any particular time has developed. Briefly, the cycle occurs because there are alternating periods of excessive or inadequate expenditure to generate income and so provide further expenditure....

Some 70% of total expenditure comprises consumer expenditure by the 45m-odd consumers, excluding the very young, sick and the very old. Surprisingly this expenditure does not change significantly; it is the expenditure on gross domestic fixed capital formation which can change abruptly and, especially, the levels of stocks in warehouses and of work-in-progress. Governments, too, can be fickle in their expenditure programmes. Exports and imports can vary substantially, particularly if they are of raw materials.

5.2 How the cycle can be evened out

What is needed is some form of counter-cyclical activity, so that when growth rates are peaking they can be lowered somewhat and then, later, when output is not growing so rapidly, boosted. Because private business people are concerned with profit, whether it be in the short term or the long term, they are unlikely to spend money when they see no profit in it for them. The only alternative source of counter-cyclical activity is the government.

Notice that we use the word activity – not necessarily expenditure. The government can try and create conditions in which businesses find it profitable to continue to trade and even to expand, as well as increase its own expenditure. Opponents of increasing public expenditure argue frequently that all that the extra expenditure may do is simply bid up the prices of factors of production already in employment, so that it is wages and prices which rise, and not the nation's total output (gdp). This opposition is countered by arguments that the need to reduce unemployment and so stimulate growth is paramount. We shall be looking at government in greater detail in this chapter and again later in the book.

6 Unemployment of factors of production

In everyday speech, we refer to unemployment as meaning 'unemployed people' but unemployment also means idle machinery and waste land as well as 'dole queues'. However, unwanted machinery can be cut up and urban waste land grassed over, but the unemployment of men and women, young and old, is all too frequently an intractable problem. So, we will concentrate on unemployed people.

6.1 Unemployed people

During the 1920s and 1930s, the number of unemployed people in the UK never fell below 1m, a level of unemployment not reached again until the early 1970s. Since then, and particularly in the period 1979–82, unemployment has soared to around 3m. Moreover, many observers argue that the total would have touched 4m if the statistics had not been altered and if those people on special employment measures, such as the community programme and the restart scheme, had not been excluded.

Although far more people are unemployed now than were out of work at the trough of the recession in the early 1930s, the degree of hardship is a lot less because of the much higher level of benefits available from the government. This is not to say that there is no poverty, because there is, but that generally there is less than there was 50 or more years ago. A further development which has helped to maintain living standards is the extent to which women have been able to become breadwinners, especially by working part-time. Half a century ago there were not the jobs available in service industries and light manufacturing that there are now. The UK relied much more on heavy manufacturing and coal mining.

Economists classify unemployment into several categories.

Structural unemployment occurs when an industry goes into long-term decline. Examples are textiles, shipbuilding, steelmaking and coalmining. Once upon a time the West Midlands was a 'hive of industry' based on the metal trades and a booming car industry, but it is now almost as badly hit as the North East and North West. Manufacturing industry in the UK shed 2m jobs in the period 1979 to 1987 and in 1987 Spain seemed likely to make more cars than this country!

Seasonal unemployment is particularly important in the building trades, because work is difficult in very wintry weather. It is also important in seaside resorts, for similar reasons.

Frictional unemployment occurs when people change jobs and spend two or three weeks searching. Unhappily, the period between jobs is now much more likely to be at least two or three months in many areas away from the ever-booming South East.

Cyclical unemployment is due to the business cycle but some argue that it is difficult to distinguish from structural unemployment because the downturn in the business cycle will accentuate a structural decline in important industries such as motor car manfacturing.

6.2 Unemployment v. inflation

Some economists have argued that governments have a choice: either unemployment and low inflation or less unemployment and higher rates of inflation. In the late 1950s, Professor Phillips published a curve showing the relationship between unemployment and wage inflation for the period 1861 to 1957 – almost a century. This Phillips curve was somewhat like a demand curve in shape, except that it crossed the horizontal scale in the bottom right-hand of the diagram (*see* Fig. 4.1).

Notice that the vertical scale becomes negative, and that unemployment is expressed as a percentage of the total working population (in 1987 it was about 12%).

However, by 1967 unemployment and inflation began to rise together; this is called *stagflation*. It was then argued that workers sought not just rises in money wages but increases in real wages, i.e. after allowing for price rises.

For individual firms, industries and, in a competitive world, individual economies, it is quite possible for workers to price themselves out of jobs. Fleet Street is a prime example, where high wages and restrictive numbers of workers per machine enshrined in long-standing agreements between unions and

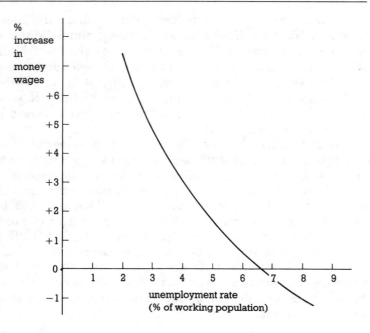

Fig. 4.1 The Phillips curve

management have forced the employers to move the printing of newspapers to new sites.

6.3 Unemployment and banking

Fortunately, most bank employees have never known unemployment, although there have been some redundancies in banks in the City of London. However, nearly all those affected were able to join other banks quite rapidly. Relatively strong unions have been able to secure no redundancy clauses in some surveys of staffing levels but not in the comprehensive reviews of branch structures due to be undertaken in the late 1980s.

For the time being, therefore, bank employees are likely to be affected only indirectly by unemployment, as it affects the business of their branches.

Government financial support for redundant workers is now much higher than it was two generations ago. Moreover, many employers, such as British Steel, British Coal and ICI, have been able to offer very generous terms for workers prepared to accept voluntary severance or early retirement. These large cash

state retirement pensions, to the RPI helps to alleviate the effects of inflation.

Gdp is the UK's total output of goods and services. It can be measured by the final expenditure on the output, by the income of factors of production earned in producing it and by the net output of firms and industries, i.e. output less inputs.

The business cycle still causes booms and depressions and governments must choose whether to aim for curbing inflation or reducing unemployment. To achieve these goals they can use monetary policy, influencing the money supply, interest rates and the exchange rate. They can also use fiscal policy, involving their expenditure, revenue and borrowing.

Questions

1 In which of the three ways of measuring gdp, if any, do the following appear:
  (a) your salary as a bank employee;
  (b) your day-to-day expenditure;
  (c) your grandparents' state retirement pensions?
2 What are the major goals of economic policy pursued by governments of OECD countries?
3 By what policies do they try to achieve these goals?
4 Are some of the goals and the policies inter-dependent, if not contradictory?
5 What is likely to be the effect on gdp of an increase in the number of nannies paid to look after young children and doing work formerly done freely by wives?
6 Explain, in ordinary language, what are meant by the accelerator and the multiplier.
7 Should governments control the wage increases which employers may pay, in particular your annual salary increa
8 Should governments control price increases, by requiring manufacturers to obtain permission from a 'Price Control Commission' before prices are raised?
9 Should governments have regulations to govern working conditions in factories, mines, transport, shops, warehouses and offices?
10 What are the various headings of expenditure used to calculate gdp? In what ways do banks finance this expenditure?
11 What are the various categories of income used to calculate

gdp? What bank savings products can be sold to the factors of production (or their owners) receiving this income?

12 What are 'transfer payments' and why are they excluded from the calculations of gdp? What bank products can be used to facilitate these payments?

13 If all state retirement pensions are paid only to bank or building society accounts, what is the likely effect on the bank accounts of all the 20 000-odd sub-post offices?

14 Make a guess as to your salary in 10 years' time. How much of the increase do you think will be due to your likely promotion and scale rises and how much to inflation?

15 Try and calculate your own 'marginal propensity to consume'. What percentage is it of your marginal pound of income?

16 If the bank were to pay you a windfall bonus of (say) £300, how would you divide it between spending, saving or giving cash to relatives (buying presents is spending)?

17 If you lost your job because your branch was down-graded or closed, where would you seek other employment?

18 Imagine you are 20 years older. How would you come to terms with unemployment at the age of about 40?

19 If rationing were introduced in time of extreme crisis, would you buy extra goods on the black market?

20 What is the most expensive item (car, holiday) which you have ever bought? Did you have any financial help in paying for it (gift/loan from parents, bank loan, HP, etc.)? In which expenditure category of gdp did it feature?

5
Banks

1 Objectives

When you have studied this chapter you should:
1 know the various types of banks;
2 know the financial markets in which they operate;
3 have an outline knowledge of the products designed to be sold on these markets;
4 know the banks' principal competitors in these markets and how banks and competitors are adapting in the face of this competition;
5 appreciate the significance of interest rates, particularly when compared to inflation;
6 be aware of the wide range of interest rates – ranging from minimal rates on current account credit balances to those levied on unauthorised overdrafts.

2 Introduction

In this chapter we look at the work of banks and their competitors, not at branch level but rather as financial firms operating in their various markets. This may seem strange to you, because you are probably working in a local branch which competes in the retail market for the business of personal and small business customers. Those of you who have just entered banking and who are exempt from the Preliminary Section of the Banking Certificate are strongly advised to read one of the books recommended for 'The Business of Banking' examination. Even those who have passed this examination may find it useful to read one of these books again to get a fuller picture of what banking is all about.

Because we are all very busy doing our daily routine work it is difficult to get an overall picture of how our bank is performing and changing in the competitive environment of a mixed economy. We hope that this chapter will help you.

3 Banks: the various types

First, we must answer the question: what is a bank? The economist will answer that a bank is *a financial institution whose liabilities (bank notes or deposits) are generally accepted by the community as money*. In Chapter 7 we shall see how notes and bank deposits comprise most, but not all, of what are termed the *monetary aggregates*. A non-economist would give the answer that a bank is a financial institution authorised as a bank under the Banking Act 1987. In other words it's a matter for the lawyers and you will doubtless study the Act in 'Banking: the Legal Environment'.

At the top of the banking tree, as it were, sits the Bank of England. It is the *central bank*, providing banking services to the government and to other banks as well as undertaking a host of other functions, such as printing bank notes. It does not compete with the other banks, rather it supervises them, and we shall study it in much greater detail in Chapter 10.

Most other banks in the UK are *commercial banks* of one kind or another. Classifications change from time to time but the following ones should be helpful. These are used by the Bank of England and are shown in order of size at the end of June 1987.

1 *Japanese banks*, with total liabilities of £237bn. About 90% of their deposits are in foreign currencies, so that their sterling business is still quite small. One particular niche of the market in which they have specialised is lending to local authorities.
2 *'Other overseas banks'*, which means all overseas banks except those from the USA and Japan. They comprise banks from EEC countries, from Canada, Australia, Hong Kong, South America and the Middle East, as well as many other countries. They too, have most of their deposits in foreign currencies, out of £233bn in liabilities.
3 Very close behind come the *retail banks*, with £231bn, comprising largely the London and Scottish clearing banks, which now include the TSB. Also in this category are the Yorkshire Bank and the Co-operative Bank. Only some 20–25% of their deposits are in foreign currencies, so that if we were considering

solely sterling deposits then the retail banks would be far ahead of all the other banks.

4 *American banks*, with liabilities of £100bn, were formerly more important, but they have been completely overtaken by the Japanese banks. Some 80% of their deposits are in foreign currencies but twenty years ago they provided stiff competition for the clearing banks' sterling business with UK companies.

5 *Other British banks*, with liabilities of £78bn; only about 33% of their deposits are in sterling. Standard Chartered is in this category

6 *Accepting houses* are the old established merchant banks, members of the Accepting Houses Committee. An *acceptance* is a bill of exchange which has been endorsed by the bank, and if this bank is a member of the Accepting Houses Committee then the bill can be sold for a better price than if the bank were not so highly regarded. Barings and Lazards are two of the most famous of these merchant banks. It has been said that 'merchant banks live on their wits, clearing banks on their deposits'. This comment is borne out by the relatively small size of their deposits, £35bn, of which about 33% are in foreign exchange.

7 *Consortium banks* are those which are owned by two or more other banks at least. They were not very active in the mid-1980s, because owning banks, one of which is an overseas bank, now prefer to do the business in their own name and so their deposits, of which 75% are in foreign currencies, total only £17bn.

Please notice the importance of deposits in currencies other than the pound sterling. During the past 30 years London became the world's leading centre for this type of business, which is largely in US dollars. Some large branches of retail (High Street) banks maintain such accounts, known as *retained currency accounts*, for important company customers, but the majority are maintained in the treasury departments at the banks' head offices.

Savings banks are no longer important in the UK, now that the TSB has become a commercial bank with its shares quoted on the stock exchange. They differ from commercial banks in that their prime function is to receive deposits, which are then on-lent to the government; they do not lend to the private sector. The *National Savings Bank* is the major example, with two main products: the ordinary account, with two rates of interest, the first £70 of which each year is free of income tax, and the investment account (INVAC). Balances in INVAC are subject to one month's notice of withdrawal but they receive a relatively high rate of interest which, like interest on the ordinary account, is paid gross of tax. All interest from INVAC is subject to income tax, so depositors must declare it on their tax returns. The National Savings Bank is not regarded as a bank for many of the statistics of money supply.

3.1 Non-bank financial intermediaries

This is a too long phrase; we shall shorten it to NBFIs. They comprise a whole range of institutions, such as building societies, insurance companies, pension funds, unit trusts, which take money in now and pay it out later, either when we ask for it or when a life insurance policy matures. They are very large, as the following statistics show:

1 *Pension funds*, with assets approaching £175bn, are the largest.
2 *Building societies*, with about £150bn, mostly funded from their branch network.
3 *Insurance companies* are about the same size (£150bn).
4 *Unit trusts* and *investment trusts* are much smaller.

3.2 What do banks and NBFIs do?

Their major function is to channel finance from borrowers to lenders and then channel it back again. You can see this occurring in your branch; elderly customers may have substantial credit balances and the young marrieds may have low credit balances, substantial home loans and personal loans as well. In effect: your branch lends the elderly customers' deposits to the young marrieds. But you may not have realised that life insurance companies, for instance, do much the same thing. They invest our premiums in government securities, ordinary shares and property and then credit us with part of the income in the form of bonuses, declared every year. In principle, it's like a deposit account, except that it might be costly to withdraw your savings. However, you can borrow from the insurance company on the strength of the premiums you have already paid.

Unit trusts invest in shares, and they show the rises and falls of the shares they own as changes in the prices of their units. Only a few provide loan facilities of up to half the value of a unit-holder's holding but they all buy the units back from us fairly quickly. Unlike insurance companies, they do not usually invest in government securities or property.

Pension funds are also much the same sort of intermediaries as insurance companies. Although they do not lend to members in the same way as life insurance companies are prepared to lend to their policy-holders, some of them are involved in a fast-growing new product called the *pension mortgage*. Under a pension mortgage you borrow from a bank or building society to buy a house but the bulk of the finance to repay the principal sum borrowed comes from the lump sum (the commutation) which you can elect to receive when you cease working. Obviously, interest has to be paid in the meantime on the loan which is provided by a building society, bank or insurance company.

So, we can see that financial institutions channel funds from 'surplus units' (you and me on pay day!) to 'deficit units' (you and me the week before pay day!). Sometimes they channel the money from people to people, as building societies have done for many years, and sometimes from people to firms (the economists' definition of a firm), or firm to firm or people and firms to the government. This process is called *financial intermediation* and then banks and NBFIs are termed *financial intermediaries*.

Occasionally, the lenders and borrowers contact each other directly (as when we buy shares in BP or ICI – or lend money to a relative). This process is called *disintermediation*.

To use even more jargon, banks and NBFIs have been diversifying and intermingling. The banks' profits have been susceptible to changes in interest rates, so they have begun to branch out into what are termed *non-funds based products*. Unit trusts and insurance policies are two such examples – anything where the income is in the form of a fee or commission or service charge rather than interest. Similarly, the NBFIs have noticed the high profits of banks when the margin between interest charged and interest paid is wide and they have begun to encroach on the banks' 'core business' of lending and also providing cheque facilities.

In particular, the *building societies* have begun to provide cheque accounts, insurance, personal loans and credit cards, now that the Building Societies Act 1986 is force. Indeed, some now have their own sort code numbers just like banks. People can have their salaries paid directly to a building society account on which they can draw cheques.

To some extent, therefore, the economist's definition of a bank, which we gave earlier, must now be extended to building societies, whose shares and deposits now feature in several of the monetary aggregates.

4 Financial markets

At one time, banks and NBFIs could picture their markets geographically. A branch of a bank or building society in, say, Derby would not wish to compete in, say, Nottingham. Their own branch there could handle the business. There were exceptions, because distant customers could always use the post and cash cheques at a local branch. And there was always the discount market in the City of London, which handles funds from all over the country.

But, recently, markets have begun to become structured according to the size of the sums involved and the nature of the products being sold. Regional branches have been established to handle trust and investment business (these date back many years), international business, large corporate customers such as the ICIs and BPs who are serviced from London generally, and more recently the medium-sized commercial firms, with annual sales exceeding, perhaps, £½m.

4.1 Retail markets

These are the concern of the majority of bank and building society branches, i.e. the High Street branches. The markets can be sub-divided into:

1 *personal* – individuals, families and clubs and associations. Further sub-divisions include students, young marrieds and the elderly, and special products have been devised for these groups, e.g. student accounts, budget (revolving loan facility) accounts and free banking for the over-55s. But all these products are sold by every branch, and this is a characteristic of much of the personal banking market. Formalised sub-markets do exist:

(a) *high net worth individuals*, i.e. rich people, who are sold products either from regional branches or from the most famous private bank, i.e. Coutts, the Nat West subsidiary which provides banking services to the royal family;

(b) *expatriates* are those working and living abroad for a spell but who maintain close links with the UK. These customers have special tax problems and are sold products by bank officials who fly out to the Gulf – which is where much of the business is located.

Most of the expatriates maintain accounts at branches in the Channel Islands or the Isle of Man, to be outside the tax system of the UK.

All personal customers now have a published tariff of charges to which they can refer and they are wooed with a range of products, from current accounts to credit cards, home loans, personal loans and share dealing accounts.

2 *commercial*, ranging from the local newsagent to firms with sales of up to £500 000 pa (£10 000 per week). Their charges are assessed on a different tariff because of the nature of the work which the branch does for them. For instance, shopkeepers will pay in bulky credits of cash and cheques, while surveillance of their accounts will involve technical balance sheet and cash flow analysis.

Their banking products, too, are very different in detail from those for personal customers. In particular, banks have devised special loans for small businesses, although criticism has been made of the difficulties claimed by some business people that banks want excessive security from them when they are setting up and have no proven track record.

4.2 Wholesale markets

It is here that we see those foreign currency deposits which we came across in Section 3. The total bank deposits, including deposits *between* banks, in the UK in mid-1987 were approaching £1 trillion. Using the now universal American usage, that is £1000bn (or £1 million millions), which is a lot of money! Of this total, some £750bn is in foreign currencies, deposited and lent on the wholesale markets, where deals are done by telephone rather than face-to-face (at the counters of High Street banks). Of course, they are confirmed in writing. The minimum amount is $50 000 or £50 000, and the average amounts are much larger. The transactions are unsecured, so that banks rely on the reputation and the standing of their fellow banks. But there is one exception to this, i.e. the discount market.

The function of these markets is to enable the members – mainly banks, but also including large companies, local authorities and the central government – to adjust their liquidity positions. Banks use it as a marginal source of deposits for funding their assets, as we shall see in the next chapter.

The London discount market
This comprises the Bank of England, the discount houses which are the eight members of the London Discount Market Association and the clearing and other banks who lend the houses money against the security of bills and other assets. The total outstanding in the market is about £10bn, of which the bulk is in sterling.

The discount houses buy various bills and other financial instruments at a discount and can then hold them until maturity. If a bill is for £100 000 to be paid in three months' time then a house may buy it now for £97 500. When the bill is paid on maturity in three months' time the house will have earned £2500 on its outlay of £97 500. This is slightly over 10% pa.

However, the house can borrow perhaps £92 000 from a bank by handing over the bill as security. The difference between the loan and the face value of the bill is known as the *margin*, which is a third meaning of that word!. It can then discount further bills.

In the last century, commercial bills of exchange drawn by partnerships and, later, companies, were the core business of the market. In 1877 the Treasury bill was invented, by which the government could borrow from the market for three months in the same way as commercial firms did. For much of this century the Treasury bill was the market's core business and commercial bills fell into disuse. But since 1976 there has been a great revival of commercial bills and a decline in Treasury bills.

In the mid-1980s the core business of the discount market has been the commercial bill. In June 1987 Treasury bills discounted were only £½bn, which was a much higher total than two or three years previously, while commercial bills totalled £5bn. If a commercial bill has been 'accepted' (endorsed) by a bank recognised by the Bank of England it is known as a bank bill; if not, it is known as a trade bill.

Of the remaining business, some £2.5bn was in the form of certificates of deposit (CDs) which are, in essence, promissory notes issued and traded by commercial banks. We shall examine them in greater detail in the next chapter.

The discount market is unique, not only because it is the only wholesale market in secured money, but also because it is the only wholesale money market in which the Bank of England is active. The foreign exchange market is the other financial market in which the Bank of England operates but it is not a *lending* and *borrowing* market but one of *buyers* and *sellers*. The Bank intervenes in the discount market in its role of *lender of last resort* to the commercial banks. When short of liquid assets they will call in their loans to the discount market. If the houses find that other banks are unable to lend them the funds they need then they will turn to the Bank of England, which will lend it to them. The Bank also signals its wishes for the future trend of interest rates, as we shall see in Chapter 10. And because there are so few Treasury bills, it operates by buying and selling commercial bills.

The inter-bank market

This market's name describes its members, i.e. solely the commercial banks. What it does not tell us is that it is sub-divided into the various currencies – mainly sterling and the US dollar – that the deposits and loans are unsecured, that the sums involved are very large, although this should be evident from its wholesale nature, and that there is no lender of last resort. Its interest rates are used as yardsticks of market trends much more than those in the traditional discount market. The inter-bank market is the premier money market with about £150bn of deposits.

Other wholesale markets

1 *Certificates of deposit (CDs)* Commercial banks issue CDs for periods of from three months to two years, acknowledging the deposit of the sum stated. The holder does not have the right to 'call' his deposit (demand repayment) but may sell it for cash in a 'secondary market'. Surprisingly to an outsider, the buyer of the CD is likely to be another bank, which will include it as one of its liquid or short-term assets. Accordingly, CDs can appear on both sides of a bank's balance sheet. Those which it has issued will be part of its liabilities and those of other banks which it has purchased will appear on the assets side. If it buys one of its own CDs, it will cancel it, the contra being the cash paid out to buy it. They are issued in both sterling and US dollars.

2 *Local authorities* have a special market, in which they can borrow short-term funds pending the receipt of rate revenues, many of which are paid half-yearly. Historically, this market is older than the inter-bank market, dating from the early 1950s, when local authorities were freed from the requirement of having

to borrow solely from the central government. There is a sub-market in bonds which are loans to local authorities of up to about two years.

3 The *inter-company market* is where companies lend and borrow directly among themselves, rather than using banks. This is the technique known as *disintermediation*, because the companies are short-circuiting the financial intermediaries.

4 To some extent the inter-company market has been superseded by the *sterling commercial paper market* which began in the spring of 1986. On this market companies issue 'paper' which is akin to Treasury bills or CDs – IOUs in effect – which can be bought and sold. The commercial banks have taken advantage of the trend towards disintermediation because they help in launching 'paper' and 'make a market' in it (guarantee to buy and sell it at the market price).

5 The *Euro-commercial paper market* includes paper issued in not only European currencies but also the US dollar and the yen. Some UK companies take part in it but the majority are foreign. Its success prompted the Bank of England to initiate its sterling equivalent.

5 Interest rates

An interest rate is the price of that particular sum of money and, although economists talk glibly about the rate of interest, there are in fact a great deal. A clearing bank may pay 3% pa on branch seven-day deposits but could charge 25% pa on unauthorised overdrafts. The period of the loan can vary from overnight in the inter-bank market to ten years for a loan to finance a power station or a ship.

The reasons for this wide spectrum of interest rates are many. They include the period of the loan, the security (if any) offered, the nature of the borrower, the nature of the lender (HP companies charge more than banks because they cannot borrow to finance the loan as cheaply as banks) and the purpose of the loan (export projects traditionally attract a lower rate of interest than, say, loans for second homes). Even the size of the loan can affect the rate. In the past, many of the interest rates charged by clearing banks for lending money have been linked to their base rates. For instance, a reputable business customer might be charged 2% pa over base rate, while a borrower with a reputation for exceeding his limits might be charged 4% pa over base.

Larger corporate customers, however, have been able to 'persuade' the banks to switch their charging from being linked to base rate, which is determined by the chief excutive of a bank or a committee of senior executives (known as an 'administered' rate) to being linked to an interest rate determined by market forces and actually paid by the bank. The rate so chosen has been the *London Inter-Bank Offered Rate* (LIBOR) which is that rate charged on the loans which the banks offer on the inter-bank market.

On home loans, the banks now quote a home loan rate which need not necessarily change when base rate changes. When banks first began to grant loans for house purchase, the interest rate was linked to base rate, whereas the building societies' rates were not. For instance, a bank might have charged 2.25% over base, while the building society charged 12½%. If base rate were 10% this translated into a home loan rate of 12¼%. This made comparisons difficult since borrowers had to know the level of base rate as well as the margin over base rate.

Some banks, scenting higher profits, have opted for monthly interest rates, e.g. instead of 12% a year, why not charge 1% a month? The bank will get its interest monthly, which is a benefit for its cash-flow, and the compound rate goes up to about 12.7%. That's a clumsy figure to conjure with, but 1% a month is so simple!

5.1 Charting interest rates

Economists, particularly those employed in the treasury departments of banks, plot interest rates on graphs. They don't compare the various levels of rates charged to different borrowers as we discussed in the previous section, but rather the rate of interest on a particular financial instrument over a period of time.

Take, for instance, the inter-bank rates on 10 September 1987. The FT showed these to be:

Overnight	$11 - 8\frac{1}{4}\%$
Seven days' notice	$9\frac{9}{16} - 9\frac{7}{16}\%$
One month	$9\frac{13}{16} - 9\frac{5}{8}\%$
Three months	$10\frac{1}{4} - 10\frac{1}{8}\%$
Six months	$10\frac{1}{2} - 10\frac{3}{8}\%$
One year	$10\frac{3}{4} - 10\frac{5}{8}\%$

The wide range on overnight money is very common, as banks balance their books. The late arrival of funds could cause banks to pay excessively to cover the gap – and then if the funds actually arrive they may have to be placed on the market at an unprofitable rate. If you ask why banks do choose to do this (and you should ask it) the answer is that it is better to earn some interest than earn nothing.

A typical yield curve is shown in Fig. 5.1.

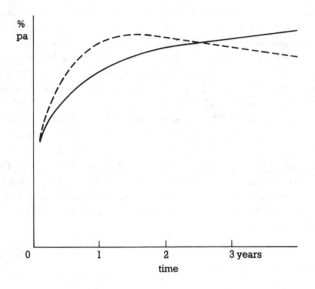

Fig. 5.1

Obviously the further we look ahead the less we can be certain and so interest rates tend to be longer. However, if we fear a crisis soon but then look forward to better times there is likely to be a hump at the beginning of the curve, as shown by the dotted line in Fig. 5.1.

5.2 Nominal and real rates of interest

If you were in business and expected, first, that the price of, say, blankets would rise 10% during the next year and, secondly, that the rate of interest you would have to pay would remain at 8%, you could borrow £10 000 to buy blankets, sell them for £11 000, pay £800 in interest to the bank and have £200 as profit.

This example illustrates how stocks can be financed reasonably when interest rates are below the rate of inflation or, at least, below the rate at which the price of the stocks increases. But in August 1987 the annual rate of inflation in the UK was 4.4%, and the base rates of the London clearing banks were 10%. So, our blanket-holders would have had to pay perhaps 13% (3% over base rate) and would have been lucky if the value of their blankets had risen by 5% over a year. They would have been out of pocket.

The rate of interest prevailing in the market is known as the *nominal rate*. After we deduct the annual rate of inflation we have the *real rate of interest*. Table 5.1 assumes that the nominal rate of interest is 12% pa and shows how rises in the annual rate of inflation will cause the real rate of interest to change from positive to negative.

Table 5.1

Inflation (% pa)	Nominal rate of interest (% pa)	Real rate of interest (% pa)
6	12	+6
8	12	+4
10	12	+2
12	12	0
14	12	−2
16	12	−4
18	12	−6

Referring back to our blanket-holder, trying to hoard blankets at a time when the rate of inflation was slightly above the rate of interest, this was in a period when the real rate of inflation was slightly negative. In August 1987, as we saw above, the real rates of interest were strongly positive, and they had been for some time. Not surprisingly, many companies were not borrowing as much from their banks as the latter would have wished.

Because so much of the banks' costs comprise nominal interest paid on deposits, as we saw earlier, the real rate of interest is not so important to them as to their customers. But if the customers begin to borrow substantially from the banks when real interest rates become negative then the banks will have to resort to the inter-bank market as their source of marginal deposits. The inter-bank rate is the marginal cost of funds to banks. In other words, the *indirect* effects of negative real interest rates can be serious for banks, as they seek to finance the loans and overdrafts requested by their customers. Likewise, when real interest rates are positive, as they have been in the mid-1980s, the banks tend to be 'under-lent' and actively seek to lend. Hence their great interest in home loans at this time.

Purists will note that we have excluded the effects of taxation, which can lower the nominal rate of interest because businesses can claim tax relief on all interest paid although we are restricted to interest paid on loans of up to £30 000 for house purchase. However, we all are liable to pay tax on interest received. After income tax at 27% is allowed for, an interest rate of 12% becomes 8.76%, so that the real rate of interest could become negative if the inflation rate rose to 9% pa.

5.3 'True' rates of interest

Do you remember our bank charging 1% a month, instead of 12% pa? We mentioned that the compound rate of interest was somewhat more than 12%, and more like 12.7%. This 12.7% is the 'true' annualised rate of interest for that particular lending product.

Now let's turn to a personal loan of, say, £1000 at a flat rate of 10%. Assume that it is to be repaid by 12 equal monthly instalments. The interest, i.e. 10% of £1000 = £100, is added to the principal to make £1100, which is then divided by 12 to give 11 monthly instalments of £91.66 and a final one of £91.74. But the *average* amount of the loan outstanding over the year is roughly £550, being half of £1000, after allowing for the capital repayments which are made at the *end* of each month. Thus the £100 of interest is actually being charged for an average loan of £550, which is the equivalent of about 18% pa in interest.

In 1974 the Consumer Credit Act was passed. It is a very complicated piece of legislation and among its provisions is the requirement that all credit transactions for sums of £15 000 or less must show an Annual Percentage Rate of charge (APR). This APR features in many advertisements and indicates the 'true' rate of interest as compared to the flat or the nominal rate. It is termed the APR of charge because it also includes fees, e.g. registration fees or credit protection insurance, which are part of the financial package to sell the item on credit.

'True' rates of interest are rarely negative in real terms; they are generally well above the rate of inflation.

As regards interest *received* by customers on their deposits with banks, there are two features of note.

First, some savings products have interest allowed monthly or quarterly, so that the rate is compounded and annualised to enable comparisons to be made. As we saw earlier, 1% a month when compounded and annualised becomes 12.7% pa. The abbreviation for *compounded annualised rate* is CAR and it is shown for each product in the Saturday financial pages of quality newspapers.

Second, since 1985 the government has required that banks pay interest 'net of tax' to us, just as building societies have done for many years. This means that if we receive £10 each quarter in interest on our staff account with the bank then we are not liable to pay income tax at the basic rate (27% in the tax year 1987/88) on this income. However, if your income is so low that you don't pay income tax then you cannot claim a refund of the basic rate deemed to have been paid by the bank and, worse, if your marginal rate of income tax is over 27% then that £10 is 'grossed up' (£10 × $\frac{127}{100}$) to £12.70. If your marginal rate is 40% then you will be charged 13% (40% less the 27% deemed to have been paid by the bank) on £12.70 (which is £1.65).

The banks pay the income tax on the interest to the Revenue but at a slightly lower rate than the basic rate, to take into consideration that some of the banks' customers are not liable to income tax. This rate is known as the *composite* rate.

6 Competition between banks

With much of their deposits purchased on the inter-bank market, banks are in no position to compete with each other on price. The international banks and the foreign banks have quite small market shares, so that they tend to approach the conditions of perfect competition rather than oligopoly, as discussed in Chapter 3. Moreover, much of the business is syndicated or shared between the banks, with non-funds based fees being determined by the roles played at each management level of the syndicate of banks.

Retail banks, on the other hand, are much more likely to be in an oligopoly situation, with market shares of between 15% and 25% in some cases. Some retail banks, such as the Yorkshire Bank, the Co-operative Bank and those branches of Indian and Pakistani banks serving local immigrant communities, have small market shares and therefore must act more cautiously, although they may be able to count on the loyalty of their customers.

When the Bank of England signals clearly that interest rates must change, by varying the rate at which it acts as lender of last resort to the discount market, then the clearing banks move very rapidly, probably within an hour, moving their base rates as indicated by the central bank. Other rates may move, but the banks may bide their time. Building societies usually change their interest rates less frequently than banks change their base and deposit rates and so the banks try not to change their home loan rates too frequently, especially if they have to raise them. On the other hand, the banks might prefer to lower their home loan rates immediately after a clear signal from the Bank of England that rates should fall, in order to gain an edge on the competition and increase market share.

Sometimes, interest rates seem poised for a fall but there is no clear indication from the Bank of England of its intentions. Because retail banks still rely to a considerable though diminishing extent on interest-free current account credit balances for their funding, there is an *endowment element* in high interest rates which benefits their profits. They receive interest at a higher rate across, say, 93% of their assets (excluding cash and fixed-rate assets), whereas they may pay interest at the higher rate on only perhaps 73% of their deposits. Consequently, banks may be loathe to be the first to cut their base rate, because other banks may not follow. Instead, the banks may lower the interest rates on products not related to base rate or may introduce new products at the lower level of interest rates.

When deciding to change its base rate and other administered rates, a clearing bank's chief executives will take into account what the Bank of England is signalling (via its intervention in the discount market), recent movements in LIBOR, the extent to which the bank is funding its assets from the inter-bank market as compared to the retail market and, finally, what its competitors are doing. If the market leader moves, then other banks will follow. If LIBOR is falling and the bank is relying more on the retail market for its funds (where rates are relatively higher) then it may wish to cut its deposit rates and its base rate, but to reduce the administered rates on its loans by less than the cut in base rate.

Between these bursts of activity, when interest rates change, banks compete among themselves by emphasising quality of service, and generally 'packaging' their products so as to differentiate them from those of their rivals.

6.1 Competition between banks and 'non-banks'

Surprisingly, this is where the banks believe that the major threat is coming from – not from overseas banks. There are two major threats:

1 in the personal market, building societies are now providing many of the services which banks have provided in the past. Cheque books, credit cards and personal loans are now part of the product range of major building societies, some of which are already members of APACS (Association for Payment Clearing Services) and BACS (formerly Bankers Automated Clearing Services Ltd). In May 1988 the Abbey National joins the cheque and credit clearings.

2 in the corporate market, served from London, the threat comes from the *securitisation* of debt. Instead of large companies borrowing from their banks, they will issue short- and long-term securities which will be bought by banks, other companies and the various NBFIs described in Section 3.1 with the probable exception of building societies. To be able to service this need of companies to issue securities, the banks must have the resources (i.e. factors of production – labour and capital) to help the companies issue it and then to 'make a market' in it.

This blurring of the distinction between banks, and stock-brokers and jobbers is part of the very important changes brought about by the Big Bang of October 1986, since when banks have been able to buy brokers and jobbers trading on the London stock exchange. There is also a fear that the Japanese securities firms, particularly Nomura Securities, may be able to take a large share of this business and use this as a base from which to expand in the UK retail banking market.

Threats in minor markets come from accountancy firms (personal taxation products), insurance brokers (insurance) and from travel agents (banks such as the Midland and the Royal Bank of Scotland now own travel agents).

In competition with public sector financial institutions such as the National Savings Bank and National Savings Certificates the banks face products which can be very 'tax effective' for certain sectors of the market, e.g. INVAC for retired people on low incomes and for grandchildren, and National Savings Certificates for those on high marginal rates of income tax.

Finally, in the long term banks face competition from stores – in particular Marks and Spencer. In the USA, Sears Roebuck has become a major provider of financial services and 'St Michael' could follow suit, building on the customer base of more than one million of its charge cardholders. Unlike other stores, Marks and Spencer does not accept other credit cards, so that it has a very active set of cardholders. To get credit at 'Marks' they have to use the company's card. Most other stores face competition from Access, Visa and the T and E cards (travel and entertainment – Diners Club and American Express) as they try to promote their own store cards. Store cards give cardholders the chance to pre-view sales, but they cannot yet provide a cash dispenser network comparable to those available to Access or Visa. They may join a building society network.

Summary

Twenty years ago, the American banks provided the major threat to the established position of the London clearing banks. Today, the main competitors are the building societies and the field of battle is the personal market rather than large companies. Tomorrow, the competition may come from Marks and Spencer and, later, from the Japanese securities firms.

In deciding whether or not to change the prices of their products, banks watch carefully the actions of their competitors and, in particular, LIBOR and any signals from the Bank of England.

Commercial banks are grouped into seven classifications by the Bank of England: retail, Japanese, US, other overseas banks, other British banks, accepting houses and consortium banks. Taking sterling deposits only, the retail banks are the largest; when foreign currency deposits are included, the Japanese banks are the largest group in the UK. The central bank and the National Savings Bank are excluded from the data.

Banks are financial intermediaries, financing deficit units with the money deposited with them by surplus units. Financial intermediaries whose liabilities are not money, e.g. pension funds, insurance companies and building societies, are known as NBFIs.

Retail banking is found in all our high streets; wholesale banking is centred on London and overseas financial centres. To make it confusing, many retail banks also undertake wholesale business.

Money markets are where unsecured loans are made, although the discount market is the very important exception. Here the Bank of England acts as lender of last resort to the banking system.

Interest rates are many, determined by the period of the loan, its purpose, the borrower and the security offered, among other influences. When interest rates are 'adjusted' for the rate of inflation, they are known as *real* rates of interest. London Inter-Bank Offered Rate (LIBOR) is a leading indicator for the market.

Questions

In this chapter we have stressed from time to time how the contents of the book link up with some of the other subjects you are studying. Accordingly, some of these questions not only relate to earlier chapters but also involve topics which you covered last year in 'The Business of Banking'.

1 Did you ask yourself, when reading the section on the London discount market: why have there been such changes since the mid-1970s in the bills, etc., dealt with in the discount market? If the answer is 'no' or 'yes', but you didn't give the reasons! then don't worry because we shall examine the reasons in Chapter 10.

2 Explain, in everyday words to a customer, the meanings of APR and CAR.

3 'The marginal cost of funds to a commercial bank is LIBOR'. Explain.

4 Watch how rapidly some building societies turn themselves into public limited companies and see whether this change makes them more liable to be taken over by banks or whether it enables them to buy NBFIs, such as HP companies or insurance companies or brokers.

5 What is meant by oligopoly? In what ways do clearing banks behave as oligopolists when:
 (a) changing their base rates?
 (b) changing their fees on 'non-funds based products'?

6 Name six charge cards issued by stores. What competitive edge have they over Access, Visa and T and E cards? What competitive edge have these credit and T and E cards over store cards?

7 Examine how banks, building societies and insurance companies are entering the estate agency market and how the agencies seem powerless to react.

8 Compare the retail banking structure outlined in Section 4.1 with that in your bank. If your bank is small, is its 'delivery system'

for the products different? Or does your bank not sell these products?

9 Who are likely to be the banks' principal competitors in the 1990s?

10 Why is it old fashioned to write about 'joint-stock banks'?

11 Watch the development of home banking (banking by telephone linked to a central computer). Why was it pioneered in the UK by the Bank of Scotland and a somewhat small building society (the Nottingham)? (Turn back to Chapter 3 Section 8.1 where you will see something akin to this, only on price rather than product.)

12 Find out more about pension mortgages (the Saturday financial pages will feature them from time to time). Watch to see if banks feature them more prominently in their range of products.

13 Who owns the major hire purchase companies? Is this an example of vertical or horizontal integration? Are the Japanese banks moving in on any independent HP companies?

14 In which of the wholesale money markets is your bank active?

15 What shareholdings, if any, does your bank have in NBFIs? Does your branch get commission for placing business with NBFIs?

16 'A bank's costs are largely salaries and interest.' How true is this statement in an age when technology is increasingly important?

17 How informed about your bank's activities are:
   (a) your colleagues?
   (b) your customers?

18 Do you find your customers initiating requests for new products or do you have to approach them first to tell them about the options open to them?

19 Which of your bank's products are most suitable for:
   (a) students?
   (b) young marrieds – both working?
   (c) young marrieds with children – one partner working?
   (d) recently unemployed?
   (e) the over-55s?

20 Examine the annual report of your bank's pension fund and find out how it invests the assets in order to pay your pension in the year 2030 or thereabouts.

6
Banks and their finances

1 Objectives

When you have studied this chapter you should:
1 know which items feature on the assets side and which on the liabilities side of bank balance sheets;
2 appreciate the relative importance of each of these items;
3 know how each item generates either outgoings (on the liability side) or income (from assets);
4 be aware, within the limits of the information divulged by the banks, of the profits (or losses) generated in the various sections of the banks' activities and by the major product groupings;
5 be able to use the information to understand your own bank's figures, which should be published in early March after you read this chapter;
6 know the major sources of the banks' deposits and the major holders of the banks' assets.

2 Introduction

Economists, you will not be surprised to learn, have not been very accurate in their balance sheet analysis of the banking system, because their totals of assets and liabilities usually never equal each other! This is not due to poor arithmetic but to the economists turning a blind eye to the banks' capital and reserves which they have never regarded as having much importance. Be that as it may, the Bank of England is certainly very interested in the banks' capital and reserves and so should you be, as students of banking and bank employees.

On the banks' part, they have usually been slow to reveal the breakdown of their assets, liabilities and profits although matters have improved recently. Banks do give a geographical breakdown of their assets and liabilities as well as profits/losses. Divisional figures are also published by some banks. But one of the measures designed many years ago by Parliament to give more information to customers – the statutory statement displayed to the public at every place where a bank carries on business – is usually a masterpiece of non-information with possibly 95% of the liabilities comprising 'deposits' and perhaps 90% of the assets described as 'advances and other accounts'.

Consequently, we have official data, for the various types of banks described in Chapter 5, which do not add up to the same totals for assets and liabilities and which ignore capital. And for individual banks we have figures which do not correspond to those in the official statistics.

Not a very promising start to your studies, you may think. Perhaps not, but we'll try and make it as interesting and as helpful as possible.

3 Liabilities

Banks' liabilities comprise mainly deposits from customers at home and abroad, in sterling and in foreign currencies. If in foreign currencies, these are converted into sterling at the exchange rate prevailing on the day the balance sheet was compiled. CDs issued appear here.

Other liabilities include trade creditors, e.g. bills for electricity, gas, telephones, stationery supplies, just like other companies. The money owed to the Revenue for corporation tax also features as a liability.

Also treated as a liability is the credit balance on the profit and loss account, after the dividends have been paid and after any sums have been transferred to reserves.

3.1 Deposits

Economists would like to see a breakdown of deposits by sector (personal, company, bank, other financial and government) as well as by currency and geographical area. But that's asking too much! Lloyds Bank plc publishes an analysis of deposits by type. On 30 June 1987 the percentage breakdown was as in Table 6.1. Notice, first, how important the international deposits are. They are lodged in over 40 countries in which the bank has branches.

Table 6.1

	%
Domestic	
Current accounts	
Non-interest bearing	11.8
Interest bearing	5.9
Deposit and savings accounts	13.5
Time deposits	22.2
Total domestic	53.4
International	
Current accounts	
Non-interest bearing	2.0
Interest bearing	3.4
Deposit and savings accounts	4.6
Time deposits	36.6
Total international	46.6
Total deposits	100.0

Second, time deposits (both domestic and international) comprise 58.8% of the total, with the 'endowment element' of non-interest bearing current accounts totalling a lowly 13.8%. We can assume, broadly speaking, that the time deposits are mainly wholesale deposits and that the other six categories are mainly retail deposits.

3.2 Capital

Capital comprises that part of a company's liabilities which are not claimed by outsiders: people who have sold it goods, people who have lent it money (the depositors in the case of a bank) or the taxmen. Capital is what the company owes itself and its members, i.e. the shareholders.

As we have seen, economists have ignored capital, concentrating on the deposits of banks. But in the past twenty years, the need for commercial banks to have an adequate cushion of capital has become apparent to the world's leading central banks and regulatory authorities. Moreover, because international banking has worldwide ramifications, these central banks are trying to co-ordinate their requirements for the capital ratios of commercial banks.

Financial analysts, when analysing the liabilities of industrial and commercial companies, refer to a concept called *gearing*, i.e. the relationship between a firm's capital (its own funds) and the moneys borrowed from banks and other outside sources. Rules of thumb are dangerous to apply but analysts look for a ratio of between 1:1 and 1:2 between 'inside' and 'outside' finance. If they were to apply the same criteria to banks the analysts would discover that banks were very highly geared, with ratios of perhaps 1:15 between capital and deposits. When profits increase, a highly geared company has a large number of fixed-interest creditors who do not have any share in the profits which are available for the shareholders. However, when times are bad and income is falling, the highly geared company has to pay its fixed-interest creditors before any dividend can be declared from the lower profits.

This extreme dependence of borrowed money makes banks highly vulnerable to loss of confidence, particularly in the wholesale markets, where each bank sets limits, just like overdraft limits, on the outstanding deals it will tolerate with individual banks. If a bank finds the limits accorded to it by other banks are being reduced it may have difficulty in renewing deposits as they fall due.

One of the ways in which banks seek to inspire confidence in the business and financial community (apart from their reputation) is to build up their capital base. Much of the detail of the structure of a bank's capital is outside your syllabus but all who work in banks must be aware of the outlines.

On 30 June 1987, the capital resources of Lloyds Bank plc totalled £3.6bn, broken down in categories shown in Table 6.2.

Undated loan capital is highly regarded by the Bank of England and, together with the equity capital, forms what is termed *primary capital*.

Table 6.2

	£m
Issued share capital	807
Reserves	1321
Total equity	2128
Undated loan capital	1148
Dated loan capital	312
Minority interests	12
	3600

Not all the capital of our leading banks is in sterling, because many of their deposits are in other currencies. Accordingly, banks have raised loan capital in foreign currencies while some have applied for their shares to be listed on the New York and Tokyo stock exchanges. Once listings have been obtained the banks will be able to raise further capital, e.g. in dollars and yen.

Share capital is owed to the shareholders, but is payable only if the company goes into liquidation. In the meantime, the shareholders are entitled to dividends if the profits are sufficient to permit this.

Reserves are funds *on call* or on *stand-by*, representing previous years' profits not distributed to shareholders or perhaps a windfall profit from the sale of an asset. From time to time banks re-value their properties, which can be numerous for retail banks or imposing city centre buildings for wholesale banks, and any surplus over book values can be credited to reserves.

Share capital can be increased in several ways:

1 A *rights issue* inviting existing shareholders to buy new shares at an attractive price. As the shareholders pay for the new shares, so the company's cash flow improves and liquid assets rise.

2 A *scrip issue* or *capitalisation of reserves* whereby sums are transferred from reserves to share capital. In the mid-1980s Lloyds Bank has made a point of having a scrip issue each summer, in order to keep the share price relatively low. In 1987 the scrip issue was 1 for 2, i.e. one extra share for every two held. The money was transferred from reserves to issued share capital and the share price dropped from about £6 a share to £4 (you should ask yourself: Why? Draw the two supply curves!) With a scrip issue there is no change in cash flow.

3 Shares can be issued to purchase another company or part of a company. If the assets acquired include cash then the cash flow will change.

4 A recent development has been the opportunity for shareholders to take their dividends not as a cheque or credit transfer but in the form of further shares. Lloyds Bank, for example, introduced this in 1987. Cash flow benefits because no money is paid to the shareholder.

Some banks have prided themselves on raising all their capital by ploughing back their profits into reserves. Others, in particular National Westminster in 1986 and Midland in 1987, have had substantial rights issues. Midland also sold its Scottish and Irish subsidiaries in 1987, in order to generate cash and increase reserves.

4 Assets: liquidity v. profitability

There is a much wider range of items on the assets side of a bank balance sheet. Assets range from cash to advances and are usually shown in a certain order. The most liquid (and least profitable) are shown first and the least liquid (most risky and hopefully most profitable) are shown last.

Banks face an age-old problem in that they need to have enough liquid assets to meet the day-to-day demands of their customers to repay their deposits and yet they need to have profitable assets in order to pay the interest on their deposits, pay the salary bill, pay the dividend to the shareholders and still be able to tuck some money into the reserves so that the business will continue to grow. The problem is that there is no asset which is both very liquid and very profitable.

Liquidity is defined as *the ability of an asset to be turned into cash rapidly, without cost and without capital loss*. You may say that cash is the most liquid asset and you are right. However, in 1971 the Bank of England decided that cash was merely *stock in trade* and could not be counted as part of the banks' *reserve assets* as they were called. (Purists will note that reserves are credit balances and assets are debit balances and will be amazed at how something can be a debit and a credit at the same time – but then economists are impure!)

Those of you with a practical turn of mind will remark that cash may be liquid enough for emergencies but that it is also very expensive to hold. Not only is interest forgone but costly vaults and security systems have to be installed to prevent it being stolen. Cash is the only asset which costs the bank money!

Advances, regarded as the most profitable asset, are not only very illiquid (would you like to repay your car loan on demand?) but also the most risky, as the current problems over loans to the third world illustrate.

So let's look at the assets of a bank, in order of decreasing liquidity and increasing profitability. We will use the six headings shown in the accounts of Lloyds Bank for 30 June 1987.

4.1 Cash and short-term funds

These comprise at least six types of asset:

1 *Notes and coin* are mainly Bank of England notes and 'coins of the realm' but include also foreign notes and coin held in branches abroad, e.g. Canada where the bank has some 55 branches. Foreign currency held in bureaux de change is likely to be excluded from this category since depositors in the UK are not entitled to demand repayment of their sterling deposits in foreign currency.

2 *Balances at the Bank of England* and other central banks where the bank has branches. Traditionally these are regarded as cash, partly because the accounts are debited when the banks draw notes from the Bank of England. The balances are of two types:

(a) *cash ratio deposits*, which are required from all banks. They must deposit 0.45% of their 'eligible liabilities' (broadly, sterling deposits from outside the banking sector for an initial period of up to two years) and these deposits earn no interest.

(b) *operational deposits*, which are held at the Bank largely by the London and Scottish clearing banks, in order to make settlements between each other and, most importantly, *to and from the government*. Again, no interest is paid.

These balances are highly liquid but completely unremunerative.

3 *Call money* is lent to discount houses against the security of treasury bills, commercial bills and sometimes gilt-edged (*see* Section 4.3). The loans are callable instantly and are highly liquid.

4 *Money at short notice* is also lent to the discount houses but can be at 2–7 days' notice. No loss is involved but they are not as liquid as call money. However, they do yield a higher rate of interest.

5 *Treasury bills*. These have been scarce in recent years, but are are still held by banks. They can be sold instantly for approximately what the banks bought them for, but there is a slight chance that the price may have moved adversely (*see* Section 4.3).

6 *Commercial bills*. These, too, can be sold rapidly and without substantial loss. Most will be bank bills, i.e. endorsed or accepted by a bank recognised as such by the Bank of England.

4.2 Cheques in course of collection

These are the cheques drawn on other banks and collected by Lloyds Bank, which will receive the proceeds in the next two days. Obviously, these items are of great practical importance to bankers (particularly if the cheques are returned unpaid, as some will be) but they are of little concern to economists because there is a contra item in 'current, deposit and other accounts' on the opposite side of the balance sheet – namely, the Lloyds cheques cross-stamped by other banks. The two flows of cheques are roughly equal and any differences are settled by drawing cheques on the banks' operational accounts at the Bank of England.

4.3 Investments

These comprise mainly gilt-edged securities issued by HM Government, plus some issued by local authorities. They can be quite remunerative but they also fluctuate in value considerably.

Let's take a simple arithmetical example, using a stock which pays £2.50 for every £100 worth held. In jargon this is said to have a *coupon* of 2½%. But you should notice that 2½% is a low return – we can get more than that from the Post Office!

In fact, as we saw in the previous chapter, interest rates are much higher than 2½%. So, how can a stock with a 2½% coupon exist when interest rates are, say, 7½%? The answer lies in the price, which moves to equate the yield from the stock to the current level of interest rates. If I can get 7½% by buying stock on the market today then I will not buy anything with a coupon of only 2½% unless the price is so low that £100 invested will yield me £7.50, i.e. the price is £33.33 per £100 of stock.

For £100 I can buy £300 of stock at 33⅓ and this £300 of stock will provide me with (3 × £2.50) of interest, i.e. £7.50.

So, when interest rates rise, the prices of fixed-interest securities fall and vice versa. And we learn from history that interest rates rise and fall, sometimes abruptly. Accordingly, the prices of these investments can fall and rise just as abruptly. By our definition, therefore, they are not liquid, because although there is an active market in which they can be sold there is no guarantee that they cannot be sold at a loss.

Indeed, many banks and discount houses have made losses on their holdings of fixed-interest securities.

4.4 Advances and other accounts

These are the largest category of a commercial bank's assets. The loans and advances are to personal borrowers, industrial and commercial companies, NBFIs, other banks and governments around the world. We shall examine these borrowers in somewhat greater detail in Section 9, which deals with all the banks.

The section is likely to include CDs issued by other banks which have been purchased by the bank's treasury as part of its day-to-day trading. Because CDs can have a maturity of up to five years it would seem appropriate to include them here rather than under short-term assets. Moreover, because they bear a fixed rate of interest they are subject to the same kind of fluctuations in value as gilt-edged.

Foreign notes and coin held in bureaux de change (foreign currency tills as some banks call them) also fluctuate in value in line with exchange rate changes and because they have to be transported to London or even sent abroad before they can be sold they are best put into this asset category.

4.5 Trade investments

These will vary from bank to bank but could comprise a shareholding in the Yorkshire Bank, a hire purchase company, a leasing company and perhaps a stake in an estate agent. Because the balance sheet is a consolidated one, the item will not include wholly owned subsidiaries.

4.6 Premises and equipment

These describe themselves. Premises are freehold, long or short leasehold, except for those overseas where different tenures apply. As we mentioned in Section 3.2, surpluses arising on revaluations are usually credited to reserves (debit the asset, credit the liability) but short leaseholds are a depreciating rather than an appreciating asset. Equipment is very illiquid, although vital if the bank is to function effectively, and should be written down rapidly, certainly before it is replaced.

Let us see how Lloyds Bank allocated its assets on 30 June 1987 in Table 6.3.

Table 6.3

Cash and short-term funds	14.7%
Cheques in course of collection	1.7%
Investments	5.4%
Advances and other accounts	75.5%
Trade investments	0.4%
Premises and equipment	2.3%
	100.0%

4.7 Special deposits

From 1960 to 1981, the Bank of England frequently called upon banks to lodge special deposits with it, as one of its instruments of monetary control. These deposits, upon which interest was usually paid, were very illiquid and designed to squeeze banks' liquid assets. Because they have not been used since 1981, they are not discussed further.

5 Contingent liabilities

Contingent liabilities comprise those liabilities which *might* arise in the future and include liabilities on forward foreign exchange contracts and indemnities and bonds given on behalf of customers. In every case *there is a contra asset*: a sale or purchase of foreign exchange or a counter indemnity from the customer. However, losses can occur on contingent liabilities, as some banks found when performance bonds were called on contracts in the Middle East undertaken but not fulfilled by customers. In other words, the contra assets (counter indemnities) proved to be inadequate.

6 Asset management

In your studies for the Business of Banking you may have read about goldsmiths issuing receipts for gold, many of which were not presented for payment for a considerable time. The receipts were simply paid in and drawn out again, without gold being demanded. You will remember that, eventually, the goldsmiths found that they had liabilities which exceeded their stock of gold, the balance being loans to the people to whom they had lent money in the form of notes. The goldsmiths had become bankers.

These goldsmiths were managing their assets from their premises. As the gold and the receipts/notes were paid in, so their deposits rose and enabled them to create new assets. This was elementary *asset management* – a technique whereby deposits are regarded as a relatively fixed element, so that a bank must re-arrange its assets to achieve the balance between liquidity and profitability. It is a typical retail banking concept, with special departments managing cash, money market, advances, premises and investments. It was a structure very familiar to your middle-aged colleagues who joined the bank in the 1950s when the only form of deposit was what we now term a *retail deposit*.

7 Liability management

It became the vogue in the later 1960s when aggressive American banks began to compete with the London clearing banks for the business of large corporate customers. Lacking branches in the High Street, these banks had no retail deposit base and had to rely on the newly-born wholesale markets for their deposits. Their technique was to target a potential customer, call on them and, if the deal was agreed, the bank's treasury in London would bid for the necessary deposits.

The treasurer's job was to fund the loan as profitably as possible, managing the liability. Interest rates on the loan were linked to LIBOR so that the bank made a profit on the margin between the interest rates received and paid.

Since the 1960s, most banks in the UK have resorted to an increasing extent to the wholesale markets for their deposits. Perhaps 30–40% of a clearing bank's sterling deposits come from the wholesale market, in which they use the techniques of liability management pioneered by the Americans.

Even building societies are becoming dependent on the wholesale markets but they, unlike banks, have a ceiling above which they cannot tap the wholesale markets. Building societies even issue CDs and are now learning the techniques of liability management.

Moreover, the large multinationals such as ICI, Shell and General Motors, also use the concept, so that their treasury offices resemble those of banks, borrowing and lending funds and buying and selling foreign exchange.

8 Profit and loss account

The yields obtainable on the assets described earlier can be found in the financial pages of quality newspapers. For short-term assets, they appear under *money and exchanges* or *money markets*; LIBOR is termed *inter-bank*. The yields on gilts are quoted in the stock market prices under *British funds*. Base rate is displayed in branches, and the margins above it charged on advances vary from 2% to 5%. However, the margins above LIBOR are generally well below 2%, arising from the greater standing of the companies able to arrange these market-related terms with their bankers.

The interest rates paid on retail deposits are displayed in branches and are published in the personal financial pages on Saturdays.

Interest received is by far the largest source of a bank's income, as shown by the following breakdown for Lloyds Bank for the first half of 1987 in Table 6.4.

Table 6.4

	%
Interest	85.8
UK current account commissions	3.3
Other UK commissions and fees	4.0
International commissions and fees	3.4
Foreign exchange trading income	1.2
Insurance broking fees	1.1
Estate agency fees	1.0
Credit card fees	0.5
Securities losses	−0.3
	100.0

Other sources pale into insignificance against interest but their marginal effect can be seen if they can be increased at a time when interest income is falling.

Interest paid is also the largest component of expenses (*see* Table 6.5).

Table 6.5

	%
Interest	65.6
Staff costs	18.9
Premises and equipment	5.0
Specific provisions for bad and doubtful debts	3.8
Other (e.g. stationery, advertising)	6.7
	100.0

Banks pay particular attention to the *net* interest received because this registers the value of their 'turn' or differential between interest paid on deposits and earned on advances.

The operating profit for the half year was £354m but, regrettably, there were exceptional provisions for bad and doubtful debts to countries experiencing balance-of-payments difficulties. These totalled £1066m and, including other items, the profit and loss appropriation account read as shown in Table 6.6.

Table 6.6

	£m
Operating profit	354
Share of profits of associated companies	15
	369
Less exceptional provisions	−1066
Loss before taxation	−697
Taxation credit	181
Loss after taxation	−516
Dividends and minority interests	39
Loss transferred from reserves	−555

The other three large clearing banks went through similar experiences: two took the exceptional provisions into the P & L account (as shown above) and one of these had sufficiently large operating profits to still register an operating profit. The fourth passed the exceptional provision straight to reserves, without affecting the operating profit. Later, it followed the others.

9 Intermediation in practice

At the end of June 1987, the banks operating in the UK had gross deposits totalling £908.8bn. This total includes inter-bank deposits and, of course, foreign currency as well as sterling deposits (*see* Table 6.7).

Table 6.7   UK monetary sector (£bn)

| | Deposits June 1987 | | |
	Sterling	Foreign currency	Total
Gross	328.3	580.5	908.8
Inter-bank	61.8	93.7	155.5
Net	266.5	486.8	753.3

Economists net out the inter-bank deposits because they wish to examine the financial relations between the banks in the monetary sector and the rest of the economy. As employees of banks we are interested in these relations but we must recognise that inter-bank deposits are just as important to our banks as deposits from non-banks. So we are interested in gross figures as well as net.

Table 6.8 omits CDs, so that the totals do not quite reach the £753.3bn of the previous one.

9.1 Sources of deposits

Table 6.8   Deposits of monetary sector (£bn)

	Sterling	Foreign currency	Total
Public sector	7.2	0.2	7.4
Private sector			
NBFIs	39.7	17.2	56.9
Industrial and commercial companies	40.2	9.6	49.8
Personal	75.3	2.2	77.5
Total private sector	155.2	29.0	184.2
Overseas sector	43.3	454.0	497.3
Total deposits	205.7	483.2	688.9
Other liabilities			39.7
Total liabilities			728.6

9.2 Assets

Table 6.9   Assets of monetary sector (£bn)

	Sterling	Foreign currency	Total
Public sector	15.2	1.7	16.9
(of which central government	11.0)		
Private sector			
NBFIs	43.3	32.5	75.8
Industrial and commercial companies	61.3	19.9	81.2
Personal	76.9	1.2	78.1
Total private sector	181.5	53.6	235.1
Overseas sector	34.6	442.0	476.6
Total	231.3	497.3	728.6

9.3 Net positions

When we compare the assets and liabilities sector by sector we find that the *public sector* is borrowing twice as much sterling from the banks as it has deposited with them, but that its borrowings in foreign currency are a mere £1bn.

The *NBFIs* are approximately in balance in sterling, although borrowing slightly more than they have deposited.

However, they have borrowed the equivalent of £15.3bn more in foreign currencies than they have deposited.

Industrial and commercial companies are traditional heavy net borrowers from banks, with £61.3bn outstanding in sterling, compared to £40.2bn deposited. A similar position obtains in foreign currencies, with the equivalent of £19.9bn outstanding in advances and loans, as against deposits equivalent to £9.6bn.

The *personal* sector is approximately in balance, with bank deposits of £77.5bn, almost wholly in sterling, and borrowings of £78.1bn, again almost entirely in sterling. This balance is in contrast to the net deposits with banks which were a distinctive feature of this sector analysis in the mid-1960s. The steady increase in private sector borrowing which has eroded its net deposits with the monetary sector is at the root of the Bank of England's concern at the size of private sector debt in the UK.

The *overseas* sector has, to a limited extent, taken on the role of providing some of the deposits needed for assets located in the other sectors. It has net deposits of £8.7bn in sterling with the monetary sector and the equivalent of £12bn in foreign currencies. However, this £20.7bn is quite small compared to the totals in the region of £450bn. In other words, it provides finance largely for borrowers in its own sector, and only some 5% of its deposits are used to fund lending to the domestic sectors.

Summary

1 Deposits are crucial for a bank because they are the source of most of its assets. They may be retail, such as non-interest bearing current accounts and deposit and savings accounts at hundreds of branches. They may be wholesale, taken for fixed periods and in many currencies, by treasury dealers.
2 Capital is also crucial, coming largely from shareholders and from profits ploughed back into the business.
3 Assets are needed to repay the banks' depositors and to earn profits to pay the shareholders.
4 No asset can do both these tasks, so banks arrange their assets over a wide range of items, from the very liquid and unprofitable with minimal risk to the highly profitable but quite risky.
5 This way of allocating assets is called asset management and dates back to the goldsmiths.
6 Much more recent is the concept of liability management, whereby assets are deliberately funded by bidding for deposits, i.e. liabilities.
7 Industrial and commercial companies still borrow, on balance after allowing for their deposits, large sums from banks.
8 The personal sector now borrows roughly as much as it deposits with the banks.

Questions

1 Using the data of Table 6.9, which are totals for all banks, do you think that the assets of branches in the following areas would be different, and for what reasons?
    (a) Sunderland, in the industrial North East;
    (b) Bournemouth, with many retired people and many hotels;
    (c) Jersey, a tax haven;
    (d) the City of London, with few personal customers;
    (e) a town in the West of England, with mainly farming customers.

2 Repeat Question 1, but using the data of Table 6.8, for the deposits of banks in these five areas.

3 Obtain a copy of your bank's annual report and accounts and compile similar tables to 6.1, 6.2, 6.3, 6.4, 6.5 and 6.6. Are there any significant differences?

4 The accounts you have used will probably contain figures for the previous year. Are there any noticeable changes between the two years, for instance in the proportion of deposits on which no interest is paid?

5 Scottish banks still issue notes. Where do these notes appear in their balance sheets?

6 Explain the difference between liability and asset management. Are building societies likely to follow banks and concentrate more upon liability management?

7 Explain, in everyday language, what is meant by (a) nominal rates of interest; (b) real rates of interest; (c) the APR; (d) CAR. Why is the APR usually above the rate of inflation?

8 Why are banks so concerned about net interest received, after deducting interest paid?

9 If a bank has a rights issue, what will be the effects on:
(a) its share capital?
(b) its liquid assets?
(c) its capital reserves?

10 If a bank has a 'scrip issue', what will be the effects on:
(a) its share capital?
(b) its liquid assets?
(c) its capital reserves?

11 If gdp were to grow at a real rate of 6%, after allowing for inflation, what effects might this have on life in:
(a) South East England?
(b) Northern Ireland?
(c) Liverpool and Merseyside?
(d) your own area, if not in the above districts?

12 If house prices were to fall, relatively to the rate of inflation (RPI), would there be a significant increase in demand to buy houses? Or do you think that the faster house prices rise, the greater is the demand for houses?

13 What is meant by the 'endowment element' in a retail bank's profits? Is it becoming smaller, and if so, why?

14 Construct a table from newspaper advertisements showing the monthly rates of interest and APRs charged by the leading credit cards and store cards. Why should everybody pay the same rate of

interest, in view of the fact that not everybody pays the same rate on their bank overdrafts?

15 Why do industrial and commercial companies tend to be net borrowers from the banks, after allowing for their deposits?

16 If banks are charging much the same rate to most borrowers, as hinted in Question 14, does this indicate that they are losing their monopoly powers and not practising price discrimination?

17 What is meant by 'contingent liabilities'?

18 Banks are able to sell jointly loans and insurance products. Are there any products which could be sold jointly with bank deposits? For instance, in what circumstances might customers acquire a large cash sum which needs investment? What products might such 'high net worth individuals' need?

19 In what circumstances can banks offer 'deposit products' to newly-unemployed customers?

20 Should banks close branches which are consistently unprofitable?

7
Money

1 Objectives

When you have studied this chapter you should:

1 know the assets which comprise money and quasi-money;
2 know that these assets are the liabilities of the banks and NBFIs which issue them;
3 understand how the government, the banks and their customers, and people overseas can all cause changes in the money supply;
4 be aware of the contentious nature of the theories of interest rates and changes in the money supply;
5 want to know more about average balances, because they are the 'retail deposit base' on which clearing banks depend.

2 Introduction

You may be unaware that economists use money in a stricter sense than we do in everyday life. 'What's the money like in her new job?' really means 'How well or badly paid is she in her new job?' Money to an economist does not mean *pay* but rather any *asset* (not a commodity) generally acceptable in settlement of a debt.

Moreover, we may have to do some revision before beginning the chapter proper. For instance, can you recall the characteristics of money? Money must be acceptable, portable, divisible, uniform, durable and stable in value if it is to perform its functions. A cheque has most of these characteristics, with the exception of acceptability for we may not know or trust the person who signed it (*drew* it is the legal term). Moreover a cheque is not an asset but merely a legal instrument which transfers a bank deposit or bank loan from one person to another. It's the bank deposit which is money.

So many students get confused between the characteristics and the functions of money that we should stress that the characteristics, or qualities, mostly end in 'able' 'ible' or 'ity'. The functions all contain letters at the end of the alphabet:

1 Medium of exchange   UX
2 Liquid store of value   UV
3 Unit of account   UU
4 Standard of deferred payments   Y

We know that we've stressed that economics is not a memory subject but when so many slip up it might be useful to have something to help you get better marks in the exam.

3 Money: a definition

Money comprises all assets which are generally acceptable in payment of debts. In whichever way we define the money supply – and there are a number of *monetary aggregates* – the largest component comprises the deposits of banks and, in some cases, building societies. Notes and coin literally are the 'small change' of the financial system and do not concern the economist that much.

One of the problems of discussing money is that there is a wide range of assets which can perform some but not all of the functions of money. The test is to take the two major functions, i.e. medium of exchange and store of value, and decide if the asset in question is:

1 generally accepted as a medium of exchange;
2 a liquid store of value (remember, we defined *liquid* in Section 4 of the previous chapter).

Building society shares and deposits are regarded by many people as stores of value and they are quite liquid but they are only just becoming generally accepted as a medium of exchange, resulting from the building societies' provision of cheque-book facilities to some of their shares and deposits.

As a result of this blurring, building society deposits feature in only some of the UK's monetary aggregates, whereas the notes in our wallets and purses feature in all of them.

3.1 Quasi-money

This comprises those financial assets which fulfil some but not all of the four functions of money. Building society shares and deposits used to be the prime example of quasi-money but by the end of the century they will probably be regarded as part of the money supply. In the late 1980s the major quasi-money assets (apart from shares and deposits in building societies) were national savings deposits and securities (including National Savings Certificates), plus CDs and other money market instruments (bills, etc.) held outside the banking system. Together these totalled about £15bn in 1987, compared to almost ten times that figure for shares and deposits in building societies.

3.2 Money: history and future

Four or five centuries ago the money supply comprised bronze, copper and silver coins; gold was to follow later. In the seventeenth and eighteenth centuries bank notes became increasingly important while the reduction of the stamp duty on cheques to one old penny per cheque in 1855 helped to ensure that bank deposits were the principal component of the money supply by the beginning of this century.

Since about 1950 building societies' liabilities, i.e. their shares and deposits, have become increasingly important. In June 1987 they comprised about 42% of the broadest of the monetary aggregates.

Just as the rise of the cheque during the second half of last century meant that bank deposits became the crucial portion of our money supply and not notes and coin, so the development of electronic and plastic money will mean that some other financial instrument may become important and not the electronic impulses or plastic, which will merely transfer the funds from debtor to creditor. Some people believe that debit balances will become increasingly important, alongside credit balances, as a form of money, but that is a personal opinion which you are at liberty to reject. The electronics or plastic would then just transfer either debit or credit balances to settle debts: in many cases we would repay debt with another debt.

4 Measuring the money supply

It should come as no surprise that there are (mid-1987) no less
than seven ways of measuring what are strictly termed the
money aggregates (plus an eighth for good measure known as
DCE). The seven monetary aggregates are all designated with
the letter M and can be depicted as in Fig. 7.1.

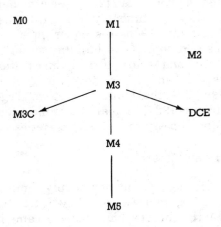

Fig. 7.1

M0 and M2 are not related to the other six and so are shown
separately. We will first outline the 'tree' of M1, M3, M4, M5
plus the 'branch' of M3C.

4.1 The narrow definition – M1

This comprises notes and coins in circulation with the general
public, i.e. excluding those in the banks' tills and cash dispensers, and sterling sight-deposits of the private sector, i.e. not
the government, with banks. Many of these sight-deposits now
attract interest, e.g. high-interest cheque accounts, and so repre-
sent money as a store of value rather than money as a medium
of exchange about to be spent on goods and services.

4.2 The broad definitions – M3, M3C, M4 and M5

M3 is M1 plus time deposits, in sterling, which are money being
used as a store of value. Foreign currency deposits of the UK
private sector are added to M3 to get M3C.

Going back to M3, which has been a key indicator in the past, we add on the private sector's holdings of shares and deposits with building societies, less the societies' deposits with banks already included in M3, to get M4. It's getting complicated but the societies' holdings of M3 are substantial and we want to avoid double counting.

Finally, to get M5, we add to M4 the private sector's holdings of money market instruments (less, of course, building society holdings) and national savings deposits and securities. Remember, the private sector includes the largest public companies as well as ordinary men and women, so its holdings of money market instruments are not negligible.

4.3 Data for June 1987

	£bn	
Notes and coin in circulation with the public	13.0	
UK private sector sterling *sight* deposits		
non-interest bearing	31.3	
interest bearing	41.3	
	85.6	= M1
UK private sector sterling *time* deposits	82.6	
	168.2	= M3
UK private sector's shares and deposits with building societies	125.0	
Less building society bank deposits in M3	−11.6	
	281.6	= M4
UK private sector's money market instruments (less those of building societies)	4.7	
National savings deposits and securities	10.1	
	296.4	= M5

To get M3C we add to M3 the value of the private sector's foreign currency deposits (£29bn) to make a total of £197.2bn.

4.4 The 'wide monetary base' M0

This comprises two totals which do not correspond exactly with anything in M1, M3–5. First, it includes notes and coin in circulation outside the Bank of England, i.e. it includes those in the banks' tills and cash dispensers. Second, it includes part, and only a small part, of the banks' deposits with the Banking Department of the Bank of England – their operational deposits.

In June 1987 these comprised some £100m out of a total of £900m in bankers' deposits. The breakdown of M0 was then:

Notes and coin in circulation outside the Bank of England	£15.0bn
Banks' operational deposits	£ 0.1bn
	£15.1bn

M0 is (at September 1987) the sole 'monetary target' of the government and we shall discuss its role more fully in Chapter 10.

4.5 Transactions balances M2

This is an attempt to sweep the 'store of value' money balances away from M1 by excluding large wholesale balances. The series begins like part of M1, using cash with the non-bank public and sterling non-interest bearing sight deposits but then includes sterling *retail* interest-bearing deposits and building society retail deposits.

4.6 Domestic credit expansion (DCE)

This was used in the 1970s and tries to measure the credit made available in a period of time. The increase in M3 is adjusted for changes in sterling lending to the private sector and for the balance of payments. After 1979 the balance of payments on current account showed substantial surpluses for several years and, moreover, exchange controls were removed in that year. Consequently, the overseas sector has seen substantial increases in deposits and advances in sterling, so that the domestic sector has been dwarfed by them. Therefore DCE is no longer published.

However, if the current account does move into substantial and continuing deficits it is likely that a comparable monetary aggregate will be designed to monitor the growth of credit in the domestic economy.

5 The demand for money

This tends to be one section of the syllabus which students have little difficulty in grasping, because we all like a bit more money in our purses, wallets and bank accounts!

5.1 Transactions demand

Really, this is common sense: we need to have some money in order to buy things. Because our income comes to us weekly or monthly (or half yearly if it's in the form of dividends on shares) it is 'lumpy', whereas hardly a day goes by without us spending some money. If we look at our bank statements we will find that the number of debit entries invariably far exceeds the number of credit entries on a page. So, we need some day-to-day working balances to pay for the goods and services we know that we shall be buying before the next receipt of income.

5.2 Precautionary demand

During the next year or so we suspect that some nasty events will occur: the car may break down or the pipes burst in our house but we don't know exactly when or where these disasters may occur. Accordingly we have a reserve of money which we try not to touch unless we really have to. Now, some of you may say that you don't do this at all because your credit card enables you to draw cash to pay the plumber or the garage. This may be true, and also shows how habits are changing, but many people still keep money for that 'rainy day'.

5.3 Speculative demand

Do you remember in Chapter 6, Section 4.3 that we saw how the price of fixed-interest investments rose and fell in the opposite way to changes in the rate of interest? Well, economists argue that one way of avoiding the loss in value of these investments is to sell them when interest rates are low and about to rise, i.e. prices are high and about to fall, and buy again at the lower price.

In other words, we are speculating with our money on the chances of a rise in interest rates. The rich investor may sell gilts and deposit the sale proceeds in a high-interest bank account. The bank clerk may transfer some of his or her staff account to a building society account or even a high-interest cheque account.

6 How money is created

Because money is a liability of the banking system – almost its sole liability, as we saw in the last chapter – one way of watching how money is created is to see how the contra items of the liabilities (the assets which are the counterpart of the increase in bank deposits) are created. Here we shall look at this process in outline; we go into it in more detail in Chapter 10. In brief, the banks' assets, and hence their liabilities, which approximate to their deposits, increase when people borrow from them. And the chief borrowers are you and me (and ICI!), the government and foreigners. Let us look at each in turn.

6.1 Private sector borrowing from the banks

This is when customers draw upon their loan accounts or increase their overdrafts to finance their spending. Most of the receipts from this expenditure will be paid into credit balances at various banks and the totals of these credit balances, which form part of the money supply, will rise accordingly. In the words of the old adage 'Every loan creates a deposit'. The truth of this can be seen when a customer draws down the loan and his or her current account is credited with the proceeds.

Now, one bank cannot 'go it alone' and create new loans and deposits on its own because its customers will spend most of the loans with traders who bank with competitor banks. The result will be a tide of cheques presented by these banks at the clearing house, and the lending bank will see its deposit at the Bank of England being rapidly depleted to pay the other banks.

Fortunately, the causes of a rise in bank lending are not at the whim of a particular general manager who wants to increase his lending but rather a widespread perception that the economic and business outlook is sufficiently promising for increased lending to be permitted by the Bank of England. As we have seen, if the Bank wanted to check the rise in lending, it could signal its intention for interest rates to rise (*see* Chapter 5, Section 6) and the rise in interest rates, which are the price of loans, should cause the demand for loans to contract.

But we must stress that it is the banking *system* which creates deposits by its increased lending rather than one bank 'going it alone'.

6.2 Government borrowing from the banks

If the government borrows money from a bank, whether by issuing a liquid Treasury bill or an illiquid gilt-edged security, it will spend the money (just like the private sector did) and the expenditure will flow to the banking system in the form of increased deposits. We saw in Chapter 6, p 94 how one bank had about 20% of its assets in liquid form (including gilt-edged): this core of liquid assets acts as a base on which banks in general can increase their lending.

Let us assume that the banking system's liquidity ratio was at the minimum level of 28% in use from 1963 to 1971 and that the government issued extra Treasury bills which it would spend on, say, aid to farmers. The banks would pay for the extra Treasury bills from their balances at the Bank of England, so not affecting their deposits from the private sector. When the farmers' bank accounts were credited with the government aid bank deposits would rise by the amount of this expenditure and liquid assets would rise by the increase in operational balances at the Bank of England. Now, if the increase in liquid assets was sufficient to raise the banks' liquidity ratios from 28% (the minimum) to say 30%, then some banks might feel confident enough to begin to increase their lending and to see a run-down in liquid assets as loans were paid over to banks which were not increasing their lending so rapidly.

We must stress here that the government is outside the banking system so that payments to it reduce bank deposits (and liquid assets) until the government spends the money again. This it usually does, but see also Chapter 10.

Notice too that this section is headed 'government borrowing *from the banks*'. If the government borrows from you and me to pay the farmers more aid all that happens is that our bank deposits fall when we lend the money and those of the farmers rise eventually. Money supply is unchanged.

6.3 External transactions

Since the end of exchange control in 1979 these have become not only massive but also very complicated. However, the sort of transaction which could increase sterling bank deposits of the UK private sector, i.e. the money supply, is a foreigner borrowing sterling in Paris (on the Euro-sterling market there) which is then on-lent to a UK resident who pays it into an account with a bank in London. Bank deposits and the money supply have both risen by the amount of the deposit. A surplus on the current account of the balance of payments will have an expansionary effect on the total of bank deposits as exporters acquire sterling with the foreign exchange they earn.

6.4 Disintermediation

This term refers to borrowers and lenders going direct to each other. If I lend you the money to buy this book, my bank account falls by the price of the book, yours rises (temporarily) and then the bookseller's rises. Money supply is unaffected but the sales of the book have risen.

Governments don't like disintermediation because economic activity can increase outside the scope of the Bank of England. If the government wants to curtail this increase which it may consider to be inflationary, then it will have to go outside the banking system to do so.

7 Interest rate theory

Previously, we have seen the wide spectrum of interest rates, some changing hourly on money and stock markets and others (the administered rates) changing far less frequently. Now we move into the realm of theory to see the ways in which economists argue that interest rates are determined.

7.1 'Real' theories

Here *real* means *non-monetary* and the interest rate acts as the price which clears the market for savings and investment (both were defined in Chapter 4). Savings are sometimes regarded as the supply of *loanable funds* and investment as the demand for these loanable funds.

7.2 Monetary theories

It was Keynes who drew people's attention to the three types of demand for money which we saw in Section 5 of this chapter. He went on to argue that it is the liquidity preference of investors which determines the price of money (the rate of interest) and that it is the speculative demand for money which fluctuates considerably, unlike the transactions and precautionary demands. Supply is fixed by the authorities.

Subsequent theorists have combined these two elements – the real and the monetary – into what are called IS–LM curves. These are diagrams very much like the scissors diagram of Chapter 2 but with different meanings. The IS curve shows the equilibrium rate of interest for the *real* market of investment (I) and savings (S) at various levels of output, while the LM curve shows the rate of interest which brings about equilibrium for the liquidity preference of investors (L) and the supply of money (M) also at various levels of output. We won't show the curves, because deriving them is quite complicated and you'll be relieved to know that you don't even need to study them for Stage 2 of the Banking Diploma!

8 The role of money

Since the early 1960s the debate has become very heated between economists of opposing views about the effect of changes in the money stock on the rest of the economy. Immediately after the end of the second world war, most economists were convinced that the money supply was not very important.

At that time it was felt that the *Quantity Theory of Money*, outlined earlier this century by Irving Fisher, had been proved to be not an equation but merely an identity, valid for whatever numbers were inserted into it. The equation was

$$MV = PT$$
where M was money supply;
V was velocity of circulation, i.e. the number of times the money stock changed hands each year;
P was the price level;
T was the total of transactions (approximating to gdp in some cases) in real terms.

The equation, when expressed in words, read that *the amount of money in an economy multiplied by the number of times it changed hands was equal to the real output of the economy times the price level.*

Opponents argued that M might change but V would probably move in the opposite direction: if M rose people wouldn't demand the extra supply of M and so V would fall as people didn't bother to spend the extra M. So nothing would happen to P or T. Others argued that there was nothing in the equation which showed whether P or T would change in response to a rise in the left-hand side.

8.1 Monetarism

Headed by Professor Milton Friedman, the monetarists have argued in the second-half of this century that money does matter. First, they say that V remains constant – the technical phrase is that there is a stable demand function for money – so that changes in M will affect the right-hand side of the equation. Second, they say that an increase in M will affect T until the economy is fully employed, when P will begin to rise. In effect, therefore, there is a grave danger that increases in M will cause P to rise, because bottlenecks in production prevent T from rising immediately.

In short, the monetarists argue that the relationship between M and T (and P) is direct, because there is a wide range of goods and services on which the increase in M can be spent.

8.2 Keynesianism

Keynesians argue that the relationship between M and T is not direct but *indirect*. An increase in M will affect the rate of interest first, causing it to fall. This fall will stimulate investment which will have multiplier effects on gdp, i.e. T. There is no stable demand for money, because demand depends largely on speculative motives, i.e. how people expect interest rates to change.

Because costs, especially wages, are rigid, attempts to reduce inflation by reducing the money supply will fail. The government should seek to restrain the growth of wages and not the growth of the monetary aggregates.

Summary

Money is, surprisingly perhaps, a somewhat vague concept, ranging from notes and coin to bank deposits and, in some circumstances, shares and deposits in building societies. Remember its two major functions, as a medium of exchange and a store of value. Be careful not to confuse its functions and its characteristics.

Monetary aggregates are measured in many ways – M1, M3–5, M0 and M2 (and M3C) in the autumn of 1987 – and the definitions of these measures are always being changed.

We demand money for spending now, for a rainy day and as an investment. Money is created when people, at home and abroad, and the government borrow from the banks in sterling.

Interest is the price of money and economic theories are based on real and monetary factors. Not surprisingly, economists disagree about the effects of increasing the money supply.

Questions

1 Why don't banks pay interest on all their deposit liabilities?

2 List the components of M0. How many of them, if any, earn interest for their holders?

3 Why do building societies pay interest on all their shares and deposits?

4 What are the capital goods industries and why do they experience severe recessions?

5 What is meant by the term 'barometric price leadership'? Why is the Cheltenham and Gloucester Building Society's Gold Star Account a good example of it?

6 'It is essentially the status of the lender rather than the method of borrowing which determines the impact of government borrowing on the money supply.' Explain.

7 Classify the main components of M4 into interest-bearing and non-interest bearing assets. Why is one of these classifications so much larger than the other?

8 What are the principal types of financial intermediaries in the UK?

9 Why is M4 likely to become an increasingly important monetary aggregate after an Act passed in 1986?

10 Why aren't cheques considered to be money?

11 What are the unique features of the discount market compared to the other wholesale money markets?

12 Name the two theories concerning interest rates.

13 Why aren't insurance *brokers* and estate agents considered to be financial intermediaries?

14 If these two groups are not financial intermediaries then why are so many financial intermediaries seeking to expand into the groups' areas of business?

15 In what sense are banks a unique type of financial intermediary? Are building societies about to perform a similar role?

16 What are the qualities needed by assets if they are to be used as money?

17 What is meant by the term 'disintermediation'? Why are the inter-company market and the sterling commercial paper market examples of disintermediation?

18 Why are there so many rates of interest in a country such as the UK?

19 What are the two major functions of money?

20 To what extent, if any, are some of the banks' deposit liabilities considered to be quasi-money rather than full money?

8
International trade and the balance of payments

1 Objectives

When you have studied this chapter, you should be able to:
1 understand why international trade occurs;
2 appreciate how important it can be in our daily lives and for our banks;
3 be aware of some of the problems involved, how governments tackle these problems and how the banks may be involved;
4 understand how nations account for their international transactions (the balance of payments);
5 be aware of how governments try to correct and finance surpluses and deficits within the total balance of payments and how banks may be involved.

2 Introduction

To get some idea of the importance of international trade in our everyday lives we should perhaps walk down our local High Street, or just look at the goods in our living rooms. In the greengrocers, there may be French apples, Egyptian potatoes, as well as bananas, oranges and lemons from tropical and semi-tropical countries. At home, the chances are that the TV, hifi, walkman and camera are all imported.

Away from the High Street, great changes have been taking place. The UK is now a net exporter not only of crude oil (thanks to the North Sea) but also of cereals (thanks to the high prices of the European Community's Common Agricultural Policy). In the North-East of England, some of the old coal staithes (wharves) are now used to load grain, following the decline of our coal exports.

We asked a bank manager how much of his business was

based on international trade. He thought for a while and replied: about 30%. Now the question which should spring to your minds is: What sort of branch did he manage? His branch was in a large suburb of Greater London, with little manufacturing industry.

3 Why trade?

The short answer may be: because we all specialise in one way or another and the division of labour is worldwide. However, such a bald statement will not earn many marks from an examiner or even from our supervisor at work. We must be more constructive and try to show how it can be beneficial for a country to produce *less* of one commodity in return for producing *more* of another.

Economists love making assumptions and international trade theory abounds with them. Some assumptions are open or declared, others are hidden. We shall state the open ones first, spend some time outlining the theory and then return to the hidden assumptions.

The open assumptions are: two countries, two commodities, complete mobility of factors of production and no transport costs.

3.1 The theory of comparative advantage

We begin by showing the output of the two commodities in each country produced by a fixed combination of factors of production, with no trade taking place. (*See* Table 8.1.)

Table 8.1

	Redland	Blueland	Total
Motor cars	300	400	700 cars
Wheat	500	100	600 bushels

It should be seen that Redland is more efficient at wheat growing and that Blueland is more efficient at making cars. So let them each specialise, with Redland transferring the factors of production (easy, isn't it in theory?) from motor cars to wheat so that it now produces 1000 bushels of wheat and no cars; Blueland switches factors in the reverse direction, ceasing to produce wheat and increasing motor car production to 800. As a result, there are an extra 400 bushels of wheat and another 100 motor cars for the inhabitants of both countries to enjoy.

The interesting feature of the theory occurs when one country is more efficient at producing *both* commodities than the other. Is it really worthwhile specialising? Let's try another table.

This time Table 8.2 will show the production as output *per unit of factors of production* combined in a fixed way (a 'bundle' of factors). Redland produces more of both commodities per 'bundle'.

Table 8.2

Per factor bundle	Redland	Blueland	Total
Motor cars	50	20	70
Wheat (bushels)	40	30	70

If we transfer three 'factor bundles' in Redland from wheat to motor cars then motor car output will rise by $3 \times 50 = 150$ cars, and wheat output will fall by $3 \times 40 = 120$ bushels.

We can then obtain these 120 bushels of wheat by transferring four 'factor bundles' in Blueland from car production to wheat. Each bundle – and there are four of them – produces 30 bushels of wheat or 20 cars, so we get our 120 bushels of wheat (4×30) by sacrificing the output of 80 (4×20) cars. But we have an extra 150 cars, so that total output is an extra 70 ($150-80$) cars.

The problem is then to find buyers for the 70 cars, or to use the surplus factors to produce something else instead of the 70 cars. But what happens if those factors cannot produce anything else?

3.2 Hidden assumptions

We have discovered one of the hidden assumptions, i.e. that all factors of production are fully employed and are likely to be fully employed. When there is not full employment the opportunity cost of producing wheat is not the cars forgone but zero. With nearly 3m people unemployed in the UK in 1987, we know only too well that this assumption is not valid.

Other hidden assumptions include the possibility for all the extra output to be sold profitably either at home or in the other country. When such surplus output is exported and sold at a loss, 'dumping' is said to occur.

Another hidden assumption is that prices (including exchange rates) are very flexible, so that they adjust rapidly to the new levels of output. But we know that prices are often slow to change, partly because of the slopes of the demand and supply curves, but also because of price agreements, including fixed exchange rates under the European Monetary System and during the 'Bretton Woods era' from 1948 to the early 1970s.

Next, the assumption of complete factor mobility within a country is unreal. Not only is it difficult to switch rapidly to producing an entirely different product but the cost schedules are unlikely to be fixed and more likely to be quite 'curvaceous', so that the ratio of one car to four bushels of wheat quickly changes to complicate the examples even further. In economists' jargon, there are no constant returns to scale.

Moreover, the supply and demand curves for cars and other manufactured goods are frequently more elastic than those for wheat and other foods and raw materials. This means that (say) a 5% change in the output of cars will be accompanied by a less than 5% change in their price, whereas a 5% change in the output of food will result in a price change of more than 5%.

4 Some problems of international trade

To be frank, unemployment caused by 'unfair competition' from overseas is seen as a very real problem by domestic manufacturers and their governments. Wages in many developing or third world countries are much lower than in the industrialised West and so 'cheap' imports, such as textiles, shoes and other manufactured goods from the third world cause great concern to established manufacturers in the industrialised countries. We are all too aware how the UK motor manufacturing industry has declined in the face of competition from Japan. There are benefits from buying these cheaper articles, as we have seen, but there are also costs involved in contracting our existing industries and these costs may outweigh, in the eyes of the government, the gains from international trade.

We have mentioned how manufactured goods may have elastic demand and supply curves, so that changes in output tend to be greater than price changes. This means that there may be problems of over- and under-capacity in the leading industrial nations. For food and raw materials, supply and demand tend to be inelastic so that price changes are more violent than output changes – and output can fluctuate quite significantly with good and bad harvests as well as labour and technical problems in the mines

Then there are tariffs, which can be imposed to raise revenue for governments, to protect domestic industry and in retaliation for a country failing to curtail exports. They act much in the same way as an additional transport cost and are a source of concern to all parties involved – exporters seeking to have them lowered and domestic competitors fearing their reduction and seeking to maintain them or even raise them.

Next come the problems of differing standards. To give some instances, different voltages are often used in domestic electrical goods, we still have some countries with right-hand drive vehicles, while differing amounts of lead are permitted by countries in goods such as petrol and toys.

Finally, there is national security. No large country welcomes the thought of being totally dependent on foreign countries for the supply of armaments, computers and other essential equipment.

4.1 How these problems are overcome

At the end of the second world war, many countries signed the General Agreement on Tariffs and Trade (GATT) which regulates trade in manufactured goods between the countries concerned. In 1987 talks began in Uruguay to extend the GATT's provisions to trade in agricultural goods (such as wheat, palm oil, coffee, cocoa, sugar and tea) and services (such as banking and insurance). In its title, GATT recognises the existence of tariffs but it has achieved a series of negotiated reductions in tariff levels during the last 40 years.

The next development is confined mainly to Europe. It is, of course, the European Economic Community which, since 1986, comprises W Germany, France, the Netherlands, Belgium, Luxembourg, Italy, the UK, Ireland, Denmark, Greece, Spain and Portugal. Morocco and Turkey have applied to join, but they are not likely to become full members until the end of the century.

The Community aims at political and economic integration of its member countries and, to this end, it has established a common external tariff which is levied on imports from outside the Community. Tariffs on trade *between* the members are being eliminated. The influence of the Community extends to 66 third world countries (the ACP countries) in Africa, the Caribbean and the Pacific, most of which were colonies when the Community was established in 1958. These ACP countries have certain privileges in their trade with the Community.

4.2 More barriers imposed by government

Apart from tariffs, there are other ways in which governments can impede the free flow of goods. The first four are called non-tariff barriers and of these the first two will be considered in the 1987 GATT round of talks.

1 *quotas*, which set a limit on the number or total value of the articles of the relevant commodity imported during a specific month, quarter or year. Because the supply is restricted, the importer or exporting manufacturer can raise the price in order to contract the demand.

2 *quality legislation* can be devised to deter imports, e.g. by requiring motor vehicle engines to emit very low quantities of exhaust, so that countries which do not have such rigid requirements for their home markets will find it expensive to make the necessary alterations to their exports. The UK imposes stringent restrictions on the import of liquid and UHT milk.

3 *voluntary export restraints (VERs)* whereby the exporting country voluntarily agrees to restrict its exports of a particular commodity to a particular country for a limited time. The attraction for the exporter is mainly this limited time, because it means that the VER will come up for review in a very short time, unlike a tariff which is likely to be imposed for an indefinite time. There is another attraction: the restriction on the quantity will enable the price to be raised. In mid-1987, the GATT did not extend to them, but they may be included in the current round of negotiations.

4 *import deposits*, which require importers to lodge a very large deposit with a bank before an import licence is granted. The deposit can be as high as 150% of the invoice value.

5 *exchange controls*. These are restrictions on the amount of money (in domestic and foreign currency) which may be taken in or out of a country and they are imposed not only on individual travellers but on all companies, partnerships and bodies seeking to remit funds into or out of a country. They usually extend to payments and receipts for goods but also for services and the remittance of interest, profits and dividends. Even if such *cur-*

rent transactions are exempt from exchange control, there may be restrictions on the movement of capital, e.g. for the purchase/sale of shares and land. The UK abolished nearly all exchange controls in 1979 and the Exchange Control Act of 1947 was repealed in May 1987.

Commercial banks were intricately involved in administering exchange control in the UK, as agents for the Bank of England. Even now, our bankers must be aware of other countries' exchange control regulations because, while it may be easy to remit funds to a country to buy an asset, it may be very difficult to bring the sale proceeds back to this country.

4.3 Where do the banks fit in?

Because nearly every country in the world has its own currency, international trade usually involves the exchange via banks of one currency for another, since the exporter can do little with the importer's currency except sell it for his or her own. However, after about 1975, the amount of trade conducted under barter (counter-trade is another word for it) arrangements has increased and many large banks now have specialised barter and counter-trade sections to act as intermediaries and handle the documents.

Also, because the parties are usually so far apart, so that the paperwork and the actual goods do not arrive together at the destination, the banks and trades have devised special products to facilitate international trade. These include documentary credits, bills of exchange, the negotiation of bills and cheques denominated in foreign currency and the collection of such bills and cheques. Negotiation means that the payee (the exporter) is credited with the proceeds forthwith, subject to being debited if the cheque/bill is dishonoured; cheques for collection are not credited to the payees' accounts until the collecting bank is satisfied that they have been paid by the bank on which they are drawn. Obviously, the charges for negotiations are higher than for collections.

International tourism is becoming increasingly important and products such as foreign currency tills (bureaux de change), travellers cheques and Eurocheques have been created to help tourists.

The benefits for the banks from these products are that many are not balance-sheet based, i.e. they do not involve assets, which require funding from deposits and which are based upon part of a bank's capital base. They all generate fees and commissions (non-funds based income) featuring only in the profit and loss account, as we saw in Chapter 6. Nevertheless, although they do not use scarce deposits or capital resources, they do require the use of skilled and expensive personnel and premises.

Some of the banks' products for international trade do involve their balance sheets, and, for instance, loans.

5 The balance of payments

Most countries publish statistics showing their *balance of international payments*. However, a word of warning is necessary because the statistics are more like a profit and loss or trading account than a balance sheet. You will remember from your studies of accounts that a balance sheet resembles a photograph taken on one special day whereas a trading or profit and loss account records the flows of transactions over a year or a quarter. A balance of payments records all transactions between one country and the rest of the world over a year or a quarter.

5.1 What does it comprise?

In short, every transaction between that country and the rest of the world is included.

1 *merchandise (visible) trade* is very closely controlled by each country's customs authorities and so the visible trade statistics are often the most readily available section of a country's balance of payments. Now, for another word of caution: the balance of payments is also a balance of payments *and receipts*. So, we need two columns: one for receipts (from exports) and a second for payments (for imports).

Unfortunately, the customs officers are only really interested in the values of goods as they cross borders – for instance, a motor car being exported from Fords at Dagenham Dock is worth much the same as one in the showrooms at (say) Birmingham. The customs are not interested in how much it will cost Fords to ship the car to (say) Norway or in how much has been paid in insurance premiums. However, economists are interested partly because the freight and insurance charges increase the car's cost to the Norwegian buyer. More important, however, is the need to know how much we are paying foreigners for freight, insurance, etc. and how much they are paying us for these items.

But when we come to look at the figures for our visible imports we find that the customs statistics *include* the freight, insurance and handling charges. In short, exports are shown *free on board* (fob) and imports are shown including *cost, insurance and freight* (cif). Accordingly, the imports are adjusted to an fob basis. This allows us to obtain a more accurate figure for 'invisibles'.

2 *services*, such as insurance, shipping, airlines, road and rail haulage are part of what are termed *invisible trade*. They include banking, authors' royalties, fees from TV programmes transmitted overseas and, especially, receipts from foreign tourists.

3 *interest, profits and dividends (IPD)* are another very important section of invisible transactions. For the UK this item is traditionally very much in our favour but for some countries, heavily in debt to foreign banks, governments and private investors, the net figure for IPD can be a substantial payment. Moreover, if much of the debt is subject to variable and not fixed interest rates, then an increase in US interest rates can cause the net payment to become larger.

4 *emigrant workers' remittances* are very important for some countries, e.g. Italy, Egypt and Lesotho, whose workers emigrate to other countries to find work.

5 *transfers* are official payments and receipts for forces stationed overseas, embassies abroad, famine relief and, for the UK since 1973, to and from the European Commission in respect of the EEC budget. For the UK, the total is invariably a deficit.

6 *current account*. This comprises all the visible and invisible items. It is defined as recording international flows of goods and services and other income to and from abroad. It does not include items of a capital nature, which are shown in a separate section of the balance of payments. Let us compile of a balance of payments on current account of an imaginary country, Gardenia (*see* Table 8.3.).

Gardenia has a visible deficit of $500m, an invisible surplus of $400m, giving it a deficit on current account of $100m. Why, you may (or should) ask, do we use dollars, rather than the Gardenia slug, as the unit of account. Well, if we used a little known currency such as the Gardenia slug, we would have difficulty in comparing Gardenia with other countries, so the

Table 8.3

	$m
Exports fob	+3500
Imports fob	−4000
Visible balance	− 500
Insurance, banking, shipping (net)	− 100
Tourism (net)	+ 600
Interest, profits, dividends (net)	− 200
Emigrants' remittances	+ 100
Current account	− 100

IMF compiles balance-of-payments data in dollars as an international unit of account, facilitating comparisons.

You may wonder why the Gardenian current account is in deficit when we are talking about a *balance* of payments. Can there be a deficit? The answer is that there can be – indeed there is likely to be – a surplus or deficit on the current account but that it will be offset exactly by the rest of the balance of payments. The debits and credits should be exactly equal and, moreover, there is even a section for 'unrecorded items' for that part of the change in reserves which can't be explained by reference to other transactions.

7 *external assets and liabilities.* There are transactions which are not connected with goods, services or income from investments and used to be known as the *capital account.* The items which comprised the capital account are quite wide-ranging but we can indicate three major categories:

(a) *direct investment* in the form of houses, shops, factories, warehouses etc.;

(b) *portfolio investment*, comprising stocks and shares;

(c) *loans*: the interest rates on these can be at concessional or commercial rates, as well as being either fixed or variable (interest payments appear in the current account).

When UK residents buy an asset abroad they can pay for it in cash: in which case the UK's gold and foreign exchange reserves will fall by the amount of the purchase price; or, they can borrow some of the purchase price: in which case the reserves fall by the amount of the deposit paid and the remainder of the asset is financed by the increase in liabilities when they obtain the loan. Any income from the asset will be used to pay interest on the loan. The income and the loan interest appear in the invisibles section of the current account: the loan drawdown and repayments are part of the capital account. However, the interest payments and capital repayments are added together to obtain the figure for *debt service*.

When we add the current account balance to the capital account we should obtain a figure which is equal to, but opposite in sign to, any change in the country's stock of foreign money (more correctly, its official holdings of gold, SDRs and foreign exchange).

Let us return to Gardenia which, because it is so nice, attracts considerable foreign investment. Table 8.4 shows the rest of the imaginary balance of payments:

Table 8.4

	$m	
Current account	−100	
Capital account	+ 200	
Overall balance	+ 100	
Change in official reserves	− 100	− = increase in a real account
	NIL	

The signs get a little confusing at this stage, but because a cash balance is a real account adding a minus item (debit) to a real account means that the balance of the real account increases ('credit the current account − debit cash' was how we recited it as bank clerks).

5.2 How does it balance?

The abrupt answer is: every debit has a credit, so it must balance. In practice, the surpluses and deficits in the various sections finance and offset each other. However, a country's gold and foreign exchange reserves are usually not that large and neither is its capacity to incur increasing amounts of debt, so that a deficit in one section (usually the current account) ought to be corrected if the economy is not to come under serious strain. If there is a surplus on the current account, there should be a corresponding deficit on the capital account or a rise in the official reserves. A capital account deficit means that a country is investing abroad: which is fine until other countries become tired of selling their assets to the surplus country's investors.

In the mid-1980s, both Japan and W Germany have large surpluses on their current accounts and are investing abroad; the USA has a very very large current account deficit and is borrowing heavily. Following the development of North Sea oil the UK had substantial surpluses on its current account and has made significant investments abroad but in 1986 the surplus became a small deficit and forecasters envisage a larger deficit by 1990. We might then have problems restraining imports and expanding exports.

5.3 Why do problems arise?

Briefly, the problems occur because it is difficult to achieve change. For example, if the visible trade balance is in substantial deficit and the invisibles and the capital account are unable to provide sufficient surpluses, the strain is taken on the official reserves of gold and foreign exchange. These are limited and so, eventually, the balance of trade must be restored to equilibrium. Export receipts must be increased and/or import payments decreased.

Because total revenue equals price times quantity, policy makers must so increase export sales without dropping prices too far in order that total revenue is raised as much as possible. Similarly, import volumes must be lowered, without prices rising so much that total import payments rise. It may be very difficult to increase export volumes – factories, farms and mines may be producing at full capacity already – while import cutbacks may be politically disastrous if consumers are unwilling to accept substantial reductions in imports of essential goods. Also, many countries depend on imports of spares and machinery to keep their factories, mines and road vehicles operating.

Another type of problem occurs when the country faces a high level of debt service which, as we have seen, comprises the repayment on capital account of loans received in the past together with the payment on current account of interest charged on these loans. In such cases, the surplus on visible trade and the remainder of the current account and the limited official reserves are unable to finance the debt service and the country has to ask its lenders for the debt to be 'rescheduled' (postponed). This, in essence, is what is called the *world debt problem*.

5.4 How can a current account deficit be financed?

1 The country can *run down its reserves*.
2 The country can *borrow* from:
   (a) the *IMF*, under one of its many facilities, but the more a country borrows from the Fund under nearly all its facilities, the greater the conditions which the IMF imposes on it;
   (b) *commercial banks*, although since 1982 this source of finance has become much less common;
   (c) *foreign governments*, in the form of export credits or loans;
   (d) its *suppliers*, in the form of extended trade credit (Nigeria financed much of its deficits in this way);
   (e) foreign *central banks*, as the UK did in the 1960s.
3 The country can *sell* some of its *assets*: factories, shares and houses which its citizens own in other countries. This is how the UK financed part of its war expenditure in 1940, before the USA joined the allies.

5.5 How can a current account deficit be corrected?

1 *Foreign exchange receipts must be increased.* If export demand is elastic, then a small fall in the price of exports should result in a large increase in the quantities sold, so that total revenue is greater at the new price. However, there must be sufficient spare capacity for the exporters to increase the quantity sold quite rapidly; if not, supplies will have to be switched from the home market and that could cause domestic prices to rise. It should also be remembered that invisible exports should also be increased.

Export promotion schemes, exhortation, and export finance facilities will all help but the general, across-the-board way to increase foreign exchange revenues is to devalue the currency. However, a 10% fall in export prices means (arithmetically) an 11.1% rise in import price (100 to 90 is a 10% fall from 100 but 100 to 111.1 (100/90 × 100) is an 11.1% rise). And this brings us to the next way of correcting a deficit.
2 *Reducing total foreign exchange payments.* This is far more easily achieved administratively than is an increase in export receipts. Import licences, tariffs, quotas, import deposits and exchange controls can all be imposed overnight, provided the

civil service can operate them and smuggling and evasion are not possible, but there are quite a number of international agreements which prevent their widespread use. The GATT is perhaps the best known of such agreements.

3 So, we are left with *devaluation of the exchange rate*, but this can have severe inflationary effects, particularly if the export drive diverts goods away from the home market. If the demand for imports is elastic, the total import payments will be greater at the lower domestic price (the earlier one), thus achieving a saving in foreign exchange.

Economists have a rule of thumb for estimating the effectiveness of a devaluation. If the average of the elasticities of demand for imports and exports is greater than 1 then the devaluation will be successful. Let's examine this a little more closely:

If export demand is elastic then it could be 1.2
If import demand is elastic then it could be 1.1
The average is then   1.15

However, if import demand is very inelastic (say 0.7) then it may outweigh the 1.2 export elasticity to give an average of 0.95. And if both demands are inelastic then by definition a devaluation will not increase net foreign exchange receipts.

6 The UK's recent experience

Traditionally, the UK always runs a deficit on its visible trade balance, with a surplus on its invisibles which may or may not offset this deficit; thus the current account has varied between a deficit and a surplus. However, the coming on stream of North Sea oil in the late 1970s, at a time of an historically high oil price, caused the trade balance to become a substantial surplus for the three years 1980–82 when it averaged £2.3bn a year with a peak of £3.4bn in 1981. Since then, oil prices have fallen dramatically and in 1986 the visible trade deficit was £8.3bn.

Invisible exports and imports are aptly named, because they are more difficult to value than merchandise trade and the UK statisticians are continually revising their estimates (*see* Table 8.5). For 1986 the revisions have been upward, so that net invisible earnings now (September 1987) cause the current account to register a deficit of only some £100m. In 1987 the deficit will be much larger.

Table 8.5 Current Account (£bn)

	1984	1985	1986	key
Exports fob	70.4	78.1	72.8	a
Imports fob	−74.8	−80.3	−81.1	b
Visible trade balance	−4.4	−2.2	−8.3	a + b
Services (net)	3.8	5.7	5.4	c
IPD (net)	4.4	3.4	5.1	d
Transfers (net)	− 2.3	−3.5	−2.3	e
Invisible balance	5.9	5.6	8.2	c + d + e
Current account	1.5	3.4	−0.1	a + b + c + d + e

In the summer of 1987, the presentation of the capital account was changed substantially. It is now called *transactions in UK external assets and liabilities* and includes changes in our official reserves, which are assets of course. The *balancing item* is a large and growing unrecorded surplus (*see* Table 8.6).

Table 8.6 Transactions in External Assets and Liabilities (£bn)

	1984	1985	1986	key
Outward (assets)				
Direct investment	− 6.1	− 8.8	−10.9	
Portfolio investment	−9.6	−18.3	−20.4	
Loans etc. to overseas	−15.9	−22.2	−55.9	
Change in official reserves etc.	+0.2	−2.5	−3.4	
	−31.4	−51.8	−90.6	f
Inward (liabilities)				
Direct investment	−0.2	4.4	5.3	
Portfolio investment	1.4	7.0	8.0	
Borrowing from overseas	23.1	32.3	67.9	
Total	24.3	43.7	81.4	g
Net transactions	−7.1	−8.1	−9.2	f + g
Balancing item	+5.6	+4.7	+9.3	(f + g) + current account

The points to stress about these tables are:
(a) see and understand how the pieces of the jigsaw fit together;
(b) have some idea of how large the items are: e.g. exports, imports, borrowing from and loans to overseas are very large;

(c) do not remember the numbers, just the signs. A minus indicates an outflow of funds or an increase in an asset; a plus denotes an inflow of funds or an increase in a liability. In any case, most of the numbers will surely change at the next revision, but most of the signs will not.

7 Where do the banks fit in?

In short, they fit nearly everywhere, because the balance of payments is concerned with finance and not just goods.

Banks will be concerned with:

1 facilitating all the payments and receipts – via SWIFT, letters of credit, collections, travellers cheques, to name but a few products;
2 earning foreign exchange in the invisibles section of the current account, from dividends from overseas subsidiaries, commissions on letters of credit, fees from company dividend payments and the net interest received (after deducting interest paid) on overseas loans;
3 making capital investments – e.g. when National Westminster bought a bank in the USA and Lloyds Bank sold its Californian subsidiary and shortly afterwards bought most of the assets of a Canadian bank.

The problem for most bank employees in the UK is that in the provinces and in the London suburbs the foreign desk is not highly regarded in the promotion ladder and most ambitious people avoid it. However, in the City of London, foreign business provides an attractive and rewarding career for able and ambitious bankers.

Summary

In this chapter we have seen how international trade is determined by the principles of comparative advantage (comparative and not absolute). We have seen how countries regulate trade and how they record it and all other financial transactions in their balances of payments. This always balances *overall*, because of the double-entry principle, but individual sections may be in substantial imbalance. Be careful to distinguish between financing an imbalance and correcting it. Remember, too, that one person's or one country's deficit is another's surplus.

Today, the USA, W Germany and Japan are the major industrial nations and the future courses of their exchange rates and their balances of payments are very important for other countries. In 1986, the USA had a huge current account deficit and a weak currency: the other two had surpluses and strong currencies.

In your studies for Banking Operations 1 you will learn more about bank products for international financial transactions.

Questions

1 How, if at all, does the principle of comparative costs help to explain the growth of vineyards in the south of England or of tourism in Bradford?

2 Which of the following imports are likely to be affected by VERs? Footwear from Taiwan; Golden Delicious apples from France; Turkish T-shirts; Polish coal; light aircraft from Brazil.

3 If I buy and drink a bottle of German beer in Munich, where does this purchase appear in the German balance of payments? If I buy another bottle of German brewed beer, but this time in Manchester, where does that transaction feature in the UK's balance of payments?

4 If the German beer is brewed under licence by a UK brewer in Nottingham, how much profit/licence fee is remitted back to Germany. Where does this item appear in the UK's balance of payments?

5 If a Japanese securities house buys shares in Rolls Royce plc, where does this transaction appear in the UK's balance of payments? In which section will the dividend payments be recorded in the UK's data and what will be the sign? What bank products are involved in (a) issuing the shares and (b) paying the dividends to overseas investors?

6 The Wimbledon tennis tournament attracts a great deal of media coverage. In which sections of the UK balance of payments do the following transactions occur and which bank products could be used to facilitate the financial side:

(a) *turnstile* receipts of £75 000 from overseas visitors;

(b) TV royalty fees of £190 000 to broadcast live from the centre court to overseas TV stations.

7 What measures can the UK take to correct (not finance) a deficit

on the current account of its balance of payments? How are the banks likely to be affected by and involved with these measures?

8 If the GATT negotiations in Uruguay succeed in removing some of the barriers to world trade in services should this help the business of the world's leading commercial banks?

9 If the UK runs a substantial deficit on its current account how can this deficit be financed? What role might the UK banks play in this finance?

10 How can a country, such as India, which has no or few foreign investments to sell, finance a deficit on its current account? What roles, if any, might be played in such finance, by:

(a) Indian banks
(b) leading commercial banks of the industrialised countries?

11 Quite a number of British people work in the Arabian Gulf. What bank products can be sold by UK banks to such expatriates?

12 If a country sells overseas assets to finance a current account deficit, how do these sales affect:

(a) the current account;
(b) the official reserves?

13 When investors in the USA, W Germany, and Japan buy shares in UK companies, how can these capital transactions be financed, if the USA has a current account deficit and Germany and Japan have current account surpluses?

14 If there were only two countries in the world, of equal size, and one had a deficit on the current account of its balance of payments, what can you deduce about the balance of payments of the other country? If the country with a current account deficit tried to correct it, would it be able to do so, bearing in mind that all the corrections would affect the other country?

15 If the world consisted of 150 countries of equal size, would this make the correction of current account deficits and surpluses easier or more difficult?

16 Assuming only three countries in the world, complete the following table which summarises their balances of payments:

$m	Blueland	Redland	Greenland
Current account	−200	?	?
Capital account	?	−300	?
Official reserves	unchanged	fall of 50	increase of ?

17 How helpful is it to a bank for its main country of operations to have a surplus on the current account of the balance of payments?

(Clue: do the world's most aggressive commercial banks come from countries with weak or strong current accounts?)

18 What are the likely consequences for the UK's current and capital accounts if the oil price were to:
   (a) double
   (b) fall by a half?

19 What factors helped the UK's current account after 1973 so that it recorded a record surplus of over £6bn in 1981?

20 Choosing the correct statistics from the following figures, compile the balance of payments of an imaginary country.

	Rbn
Net capital inflow	47
Gdp	740
Imports of goods	−370
Budget deficit	47
Net IPD	−23
Fall in official reserves	3
Total company profits	70
Loans outstanding to foreign banks	230
Exports of goods	250
Net tourist receipts	15
Other invisible exports	78

9
Foreign exchange and related markets

1 Objectives

When you have studied this chapter, you should:

1 understand how exchange rates are quoted;

2 understand the major factors determining exchange rates;

3 appreciate the close relationship between exchange rates and interest rates;

4 know that currencies are *bought* and *sold* on the foreign exchange market and that they are *deposited* and *lent* on the Euro-currency markets;

5 know how active banks are in these two markets;

6 know that Euro-currencies having nothing to do with the European Community;

7 be alert to the possibility that the UK may become a full member of the European Monetary System (EMS).

2 Introduction

In the previous chapter we mentioned exchange rates, which are the prices at which we buy and sell foreign currencies. If I want to buy Deutschemarks for my visit to the 1990 Oberammergau Passion Play, I would normally pay for them in sterling but I could pay for them in a third currency. The foreign exchange market is one where money buys other money. Since money is the *commodity* or stock-in-trade of banks we find that banks play a very active role in the market, particularly when compared to their passive or supporting role in international trade.

Today, most banks have merged their foreign exchange dealing rooms with their wholesale deposit-taking operations (both sterling and foreign currency) into a single Treasury. Although the two markets – foreign exchange and inter-bank deposit – are closely linked, we must remember that one buys and sells and the other deposits and lends.

Finally, we look briefly at the third-world debt problem which has arisen out of commercial bank lending to third world countries on the inter-bank and longer-term Euro-currency markets.

3 How exchange rates are quoted

One of the problems for beginners is that there is no universal way in which exchange rates are quoted. Mostly, they show how much of a foreign currency we get for one pound sterling, e.g. $1.50, DM3 or 250 yen. It's much the same as greengrocers who sell oranges at 9 for £1 and lemons at 8 for £1. When prices rise, they sell oranges at 8 for £1 (12.5p each compared with 11.1p) and lemons at 7 for £1. So, when the dollar rises, the rate against sterling may become $1.40 or even $1.30.

However, there are some currencies quoted the other way round, i.e. as with goods (oranges 12.5p each, rupees 17p each). And there are some countries such as Zimbabwe and South Africa where all exchange rates are quoted in this way.

During the 1970s and 1980s, three major currencies have emerged; the US dollar, the Deutschemark (of West Germany) and the Japanese yen. Others, such as the pound sterling and even the Swiss franc, have become of more limited significance. Consequently, in this book we try to give examples in these three major currencies, as well as sterling. Another point to be remembered is that the US dollar is no longer the sole benchmark or *numeraire* against which all other currencies are quoted. We also use artificial currency baskets, comprising the most important currencies.

The forward market has not grown in recent years as fast as the spot market, which is for deals for delivery today or up to two days' time. For the purposes of the subject 'Economics and the Banks' Role in the Economy', the forward market can be ignored, but it will be more important for Banking Operations 1, and even more so for Stage 2.

3.1 Who buys and sells foreign exchange?

As we would expect, banks play a major role in the markets – mainly the commercial banks but also the central banks. The latter, often upon the instigation of their governments, may intervene to buy and sell their own currencies (i.e. sell and buy foreign exchange) in order to influence the exchange rate.

But there are other players – for instance, the largest multi-national companies maintain foreign exchange dealing rooms and deposit-taking operations just like those of the banks. Here they buy and sell the currencies of the many countries in which they operate and, like the banks, try and use their holdings of currencies to achieve as great a profit as possible. Oil companies such as Shell, BP, Exxon (Esso), Mobil, Texaco, Socal (Chevron) and Gulf (which are the majors or 'seven sisters') operate in most countries and so have a need to buy and sell currencies for everyday business purposes. Along with other multinationals such as General Motors, Ford and ICI, they all have treasuries which resemble those of banks. Indeed, BP have considered establishing a banking operation.

Although most banks do not actually operate in as many countries as the largest multinationals, they do have 'correspondent banking relations' with other banks in nearly every country. Their customers will want to make payments, e.g. Italian immigrants in Australia may want to send money to their relatives in Naples. So, just like the multinationals, the banks will be buying and selling their holdings of foreign currencies in order to maximise the return on these assets, i.e. their *nostro* accounts in foreign currencies with their correspondent banks abroad. Likewise, the correspondent banks will maintain sterling accounts in London, which the UK banks call *vostro* – your – accounts, and these banks will use these accounts to buy and sell sterling.

You and I don't deal in foreign exchange, for when we go abroad we usually buy notes and coin or travellers cheques. Separate markets exist for buying and selling these products and they are of limited economic importance. However, if we cash a Eurocheque this will be negotiated through the nostro account. In the notes and coin/travellers cheque retail market on the streets of London, the UK banks face competition from a growing number of independent bureaux de change, and these may need to be regulated more closely in order to ensure that foreign tourists are not overcharged for their purchases of sterling.

Finally, in a number of centres around the world there are foreign exchange brokers who place buying and selling banks in touch with each other, for a commission. Such brokers do not deal directly with the customers of the banks. The brokers (and the banks) quote both a buying and a selling price: when the 'spread' is wide the implication is that the bank is reluctant to deal; when the spread narrows (i.e. the margins between the buying and selling rates are finer) the bank signals that it is willing to deal. Convention obliges a bank to deal at the rate it quotes but it need not deal for the amount requested. Most deals are done by telephone and many banks tape-record all telephone conversations, in order to minimise errors in processing the deals and in telexing the foreign exchange to where the buyer wants it sent. Errors can be costly, because they may result in accounts normally in credit becoming inadvertently overdrawn and runnng up debit interest.

3.2 Why is foreign exchange bought and sold?

For many reasons: people need it to buy goods and services; they have received it in payment for exports; they need it for a home overseas or because they are emigrating; to buy shares in overseas companies; to send to relatives abroad; to provide aid for victims of famine or disease; to pay interest to foreign investors; last but not least, to invest overseas for a short period because interest rates are very attractive in that particular country. Banks, and multinationals, will also seek that divergence of exchange rates between centres or over a short (15 minute) period of time which enables them to buy and sell again at a profit (a process known as *arbitrage*).

4 Why do exchange rates vary?

The obvious answer is because they are not fixed. A more precise answer is: because supply and demand are always changing, and the movements do not offset each other. Better still is: because supply and demand change in response to many different factors, such as the growth of exports compared with imports and the ability and desire to invest in other countries – but also because dealers move their foreign exchange from centre to centre with a view to achieving the highest return on their balances. The phrase 'with a view to' is used deliberately because dealers must make a judgement as to whether they expect the existing pattern of exchange rates and interest rates to continue, so that any extra interest is sufficient to offset the dealing costs.

Let us take some practical examples.

4.1 Trade flows

A US exporter sells 500 tractors to Spain. He/she will be paid in pesetas and so will sell them and buy US dollars. If more and more US exporters achieve similar successes then their purchases of US dollars (sales of their export proceeds) could move the dollar upwards against most other currencies. So, we must examine the factors which determine whether US exporters can export more:

1 their *products*: are they better than the competition?
2 their *prices*: are their costs too high back home?
3 their *selling ability*: can their local dealers clinch the deals in the local markets?
4 their *credit facilities*: are their interest charges too high compared with the competition?
5 their *after-sales service*: are spares easily obtainable at a reasonable price?

If all these factors are acting against the US exporters, then the dollar will tend to fall; if all are favourable, it will tend to rise. If some factors are favourable and some against then it is not obvious which way the dollar will move; the rate may be swayed by the other factors outlined below.

4.2 Interest rates

Suppose a multinational company has 420m yen in Tokyo, which are surplus to needs. However, in three months' time it must make a dividend payment of $30m to its US stockholders. What will it do with this money in the meantime? When will it sell the yen for dollars?
    First we must know the interest rates obtainable on three months' deposits in New York, Tokyo and other leading centres. In early June 1987, these were (for domestic currency deposits):

Tokyo	3.6% pa	London	8.5% pa
New York	5.9% pa	Frankfurt	3.7% pa

On the face of it, it would pay to move the funds to New York and earn 5.9% pa on them rather than a meagre 3.6% pa in Tokyo. But this ignores the possiblity that the exchange rate in three months' time might be so much more favourable that the profit would outweigh the 2.3% pa interest differential (5.9% less 3.6%) between the two centres. The yen stood at 140 to the dollar in early June 1987; if it rose to 130 in September then the Y 420m (by then having risen to Y 423.78m as a result of the interest received) would sell for $32.59m. The dividend could be paid, with $2.59m to spare. If the yen fell (the $ rose) to, say, 150, the Y 423.78m would sell for only $28.25m, leaving a gap of $1.75m to be financed. If the yen are sold now for 140, it will fetch $30m, which will increase to $30.44m if interest rates remain unchanged until September.

So, current interest rates are vital, as are current and expected exchange rates. Here we should note that for short periods of up to three months interest rates can be fixed by making deposits for fixed terms. However, for longer periods, investment decisions also involve taking a view on future interest rates.

4.3 Expectations

If enough dealers believe that a currency will fall during the next three months they will delay their purchases of it until later, thereby decreasing the demand for it and accentuating its decline. These decisions to delay purchases are known as *lags*, while the decisions to bring forward sales are known as *leads*. They tend to bring about the very changes which they expect.

4.4 Balance of payments data

Over the years, a balance of payments chronicles the ability of a country to attract sufficient foreign exchange – on both current and capital accounts – for it to pay its way in the world. Obviously, a balance of payments includes trade and short-term capital movements, but the regular publication of statistics does focus dealers' attention on a surplus or deficit on current account. In the mid-1980s, the American deficit and the Japanese surplus were both highlighted in this way.

4.5 Policy change

A major change in economic policy could affect tariffs, inflation, domestic interest rates, exchange control, the attitude to foreign inward investment and the country's exchange rate policy. Such changes are likely to occur after a general or presidential election in a democracy or a 'coup' in a dictatorship. However, they can occur in mid-term, as when President Nixon caused the US dollar to break from its fixed link with gold in the summer of 1971. In dictatorships, even unsuccessful coups could depress the rate.

4.7 The price of oil

This is another factor affecting expectations in foreign exchange markets. Oil is the most important single commodity traded internationally and is vital to nearly every country. Those industrial countries blessed with oil, such as the USA and the UK, tend to see their currencies appreciate when the oil price rises, while the opposite is true for importers such as Japan.

4.8 Purchasing power parity

This is a theory which states that the exchange rate between two currencies will tend to equal the ratio between the internal purchasing powers of the two currencies. If a bundle of goods and services in country A costs A\$1500 and in country B the same bundle costs B\$2000 then the rate for the A\$ will tend to be A\$1 = B\$1.333. But not all goods and services are traded between nations and there are now tremendous surges of short- and long-term capital which can swamp the exchange rate. However, the inflation rate in a country is frequently a factor influencing its interest rates and so domestic price levels are still important.

5 Fixed and floating rates

For many years, first under the gold standard and, later, during the 25-odd years of the Bretton Woods system after the end of the second world war, the greater part of international trade and finance was conducted under fixed exchange rates. Under the gold standard system, countries pegged their currencies to the price of gold, which could be freely exported and imported. If the exchange rate rose above or below the 'gold points' (the fixed gold price plus or minus the cost of shipping and insurance) it was cheaper to buy and sell gold at the fixed prices rather than buy and sell foreign exchange.

At a conference held in 1944 at Bretton Woods in the USA, the International Monetary Fund (IMF) was established, with the purpose of ensuring stable spot exchange rates and to provide limited and temporary finance to enable member countries to weather a temporary deficit on the current account of their balance of payments.

After the second world war, only the USA maintained the link with gold, at $35 an ounce until Nixon altered it in August 1971. By 1980 the price of gold had touched $800 an ounce, in a flurry of speculation, but it subsequently fell back to between $400 and $450 in the first half of 1987.

During the period 1948–71, most countries linked their currencies to the US dollar (or to sterling which in turn was linked to the dollar) and the dollar was linked to gold, so currencies were relatively stable.

The USA's break in 1971 with the $35 gold price (which had lasted since 1933) almost coincided with boom conditions for industrialised economies in 1972. The strains of adjustment proved considerable and by 1973 most countries in the industrialised west had moved to floating exchange rates, with the exception of the European Community.

The current system, which has prevailed since then, is called *managed flexibility*, which means that central banks intervene from time to time to bid up their currencies' exchange rates but not regularly and not to honour any obligation to the IMF. In the 1980s, exchange rate changes have become much more substantial, with swings of 40% or even 50% being seen over a period of two or three years. This applies particularly to the US dollar/yen rate.

5.1 Advantages and disadvantages

The era of fixed rates is regarded with affection because dealers knew that variations would be minimal; however, central banks needed considerable reserves of gold and foreign exchange to be able to buy their own currencies at fixed rates. Moreover, the need to defend the exchange rate meant that a government's freedom of action in economic policy was restricted. Not only could it not do anything which might affect sentiment, expectations and thus the demand for its currency, but it could not easily change the exchange rate as part of a package of economic policy measures. Finally, while central banks bought and sold their currencies mainly in the spot market, intervention in the forward market was far more risky and many speculators made large profits in forward deals; the losses were borne by central banks.

5.2 Over- and under-valued exchange rates

If trade flows, capital movements, interest rate differentials and relative inflation rates are all judged by observers as likely to depress a currency, so that it falls against other currencies, it is said to be 'over-valued'.

Another example is where these factors are tending to depress a currency which is pegged to the US dollar or to a currency basket (see next section). The strain is then taken not in the exchange rate but in the official reserves as people clamour to sell foreign exchange in a black market where the rate is much more favourable than the official rate. An over-valued currency means that imports cost less in domestic currency than they would if the rate were at a level where supply and demand for that currency were in balance.

When all the factors are tending to raise a currency's exchange rate over a period of time, the currency is said to be under-valued. The yen was under-valued in the mid-1980s. At any one time in a system of floating exchange rates, some currencies will be over-valued and others under-valued.

6 Currency baskets

In 1967, the *Special Drawing Right (SDR)* was created by the IMF. It is an artificial currency, comprising fixed amounts of the world's leading currencies. Originally, there were sixteen currencies in the SDR, but these proved too unwieldy and there are now five, i.e. US$, DM, yen, French franc and sterling, with their proportions changing every five years. Members of the IMF have been given SDRs in limited quantities in the early 1970s and again in the early 1980s; the use of SDRs is very restricted and they are little used in world trade. However, we should note that countries can peg their currencies to the SDR – Kenya is an example – and that the occasional issue of SDRs can top up the reserves of small countries in the third world. Moreover, some innovative banks offer deposits denominated in SDRs.

The SDR is an example of a currency *basket* or *cocktail* – an artificial combination of actual currencies – but it tends to be dominated by the US dollar, which comprises over 40% of it.

Currency baskets are also used to measure the purchasing power of currencies against a wide range of other currencies, duly weighted, and index numbers are quoted for currencies against these baskets. Such baskets are known as the *effective exchange rate*. In the Foreign Exchange section of the *Financial Times*, such an index is the *Sterling Index*, measuring sterling against a basket of leading currencies weighted according to their import-ance for the UK's export and import trade. The base for the index is the average for 1975.

6.1 The ECU and EMS

The European Community has its own currency basket – the *European Currency Unit (ECU)* – comprising the currencies of its twelve member countries. The DM plays a significant role in the ECU, which some observers have likened to a DM currency *bloc*. Although sterling features in the basket of currencies in the ECU, the UK did not immediately join the exchange rate mech-anism of the Community's *European Monetary System (EMS)*. This puts the UK in the same category as Greece, Portugal and Spain, all of whom are outside the exchange rate mechanism. And the exchange rate mechanism, whereby currencies are pegged to the ECU, and thus to each other, is at the heart of the EMS. In 1988 there is likely to be considerable debate as to whether or not the UK should be a full member of the EMS, pegging sterling to the ECU.

In 1987, changes were made to the administration of the EMS, so that a degree of surveillance of member states' economies will occur. In future, policy co-ordination should begin before cur-rencies reach their limits, so that intervention in that currency can begin as soon as possible. There will also be double the funds available in the so-called *debtor's quota*.

Although the UK does not belong fully to the EMS, it abolished exchange controls in 1979, whereas some members of the Com-munity still maintained them in the late summer of 1987. If, as the Community hopes, these members were to abolish these exchange controls, this would place most Community currencies on the same basis: free of exchange controls and fixed to each other. The major exception would be the sterling and increased pressure would be placed on the UK to join the *exchange rate mechanism* (ERM).

The real reason why the UK does not join the ERM is that it fears the possible loss of freedom of action, or sovereignty as it is termed, which would result.

7 Exchange rate policy

Countries now have a choice, whether to float their exchange rates, peg them to the SDR, to the US dollar or to some currency basket such as the ECU. Some countries choose to peg to an undisclosed basket of currencies, stated often to be composed of the currencies of their leading trading partners.

If a country manages its currency, it may then have a choice of exchange rate at which to aim. This has occurred in the UK, where the exchange rates against the dollar, yen and DM are known to be among the targets of monetary policy. However, we are still unaware of the precise target rates or zones at which the authorities (the Treasury and the Bank of England) aim to keep sterling although we believe we know the DM targets (*see* Chapter 10). We also do not know when the targets are changed.

8 Foreign exchange risk

Unlike international trade, foreign exchange business necessarily involves assets (the balances in foreign currency held with other banks at home and abroad) and consequently it needs a capital base to support these assets and deposits to fund them. However, like all business, foreign exchange business also involves risk and therefore it is closely scrutinised by banking supervisory authorities – in the UK the Bank of England.

Just like multinationals, international banks can be affected by exchange rate changes. Short-term changes may cause windfall profits or losses in the profit and loss account (*transaction effects*). Longer-term fluctuations may result in substantial valuation changes when assets and liabilities denominated in foreign currencies are converted into sterling for inclusion in the balance sheet at the end of the bank's financial year. These *translation effects* may need provisions to be made out of the profit and loss account in order that the assets and liabilities appear at the more recent sterling valuation, if the sterling has fallen since the previous balance sheet was compiled.

Exchange rates also affect our lives as citizens, because an over-valued rate can depress demand for exports and attract imports. On the other hand, a country with an undervalued currency will find exports booming and imports stagnating.

9 Foreign currency deposits

In the late 1950s, a market developed in London for deposits denominated not in sterling but in US dollars. The depositors were attracted to London because of the flexibility of the Bank of England's regulations, with no restrictions on the maximum rate of interest which could be paid. A further advantage for London was that some of the funds came from behind the Iron Curtain and the owners were wary of depositing the money in New York. These dollars were known as *Euro-dollars*, and a similar market developed in Paris, for *Euro-sterling*.

The major feature of a *Euro-currency* is that it is deposited and lent *outside its country of origin*. The *Euro-markets* are now very extensive indeed, with many sub-markets. We have noticed some in Chapter 5: the London inter-bank market and the Euro-commercial paper market. Other sub-markets cover most of the currencies of OECD countries, with maturities extending from overnight moneys to five-year bonds or longer.

Banking Certificate and other Stage 1 students do not need to study these markets in detail but they are important for Stage 2 students, especially for those studying for the International Banking Diploma. All students, however, must be aware that *Euro-currencies have nothing to do with the European Common Market.*

9.1 The debt problem

One of the attractions of London, compared to New York, for Euro-dollars was the absence of rigid controls and Euro-currency businesses have always been swift to seek new bases where supervision was expected to be lax. As well as London, Paris, Zurich and Frankfurt, important centres have developed in 'off-shore centres' such as Bahamas, the Cayman Islands and Bahrain, while Hong Kong and Singapore are flourishing centres for Asian-dollars.

The major problem has not been the collapse of a bank, although some have had to be rescued, but rather the excessive lending which was made to third-world countries, particularly

Latin America. The banks of the Western industrialised countries 're-cycled' the balance-of-payments surpluses of the oil exporters, especially those in the Middle East, to third-world countries to finance their balance-of-payments deficits. The oil exporters' surpluses were known as *petro-dollars* and were deposited with Western banks because the local banks were not large enough to receive the money. The operation made sense at the time, but the borrowers have been unable to meet the interest and capital repayments.

By 1987, the banks had lent Brazil, for instance, over $100bn, and then Brazil refused to pay the interest. Mexico, Argentina and Venezuela are also large borrowers which have 're-scheduled' their debts to commercial banks. Re-scheduling is a polite word for postponing. Other borrowers which are or have been talking to their lending banks include Poland, Rumania, Nigeria and the Philippines.

We noticed in Chapter 6 that all of the UK's Big Four banks made substantial provisions for these bad and doubtful debts in the early summer of 1987. Fortunately, the losses on the P & L accounts should not affect your 1988 'profit-sharing', because the banks intend to ask the shareholders to approve a special payment to staff instead. However, the losses do show us all how important are these Euro-currency operations, even if we do not come across them in our work in branch banking.

Summary

Foreign exchange rates are usually quoted as *currency to the £* or *currency to the $*, rather like 'apples are 5 to the £', instead of 'apples are 20p each'. This can be confusing to beginners, especially as some currencies are quoted normally.

Foreign exchange is bought and sold for trade, including invisibles or trade in services, and investment in other countries. Trade flows and interest rates in leading financial centres are powerful forces influencing supply and demand, as are dealers' expectations.

Since 1973 many currencies have been floating against each other, but the EEC have created a 'zone of monetary stability' in the European Monetary System. However, the UK is not yet a full member.

Foreign currency deposits are not bought and sold, but deposited and lent between banks and large commercial customers. A whole range of markets and products has evolved but much foreign currency lending to third-world countries is in arrears. The burden of this debt on borrowing countries' balances of payments forms the 'third-world debt problem'.

Questions

1 You're on a trip to Zimbabwe, and you've bought Z$200 at Z$4 to the £ from your bank in London. However, on going to pay the hotel bill in Harare you find that the rate for sterling is quoted at 2.5. There's been no revaluation, so why are the rates seemingly so different?

2 If sterling falls significantly in the foreign exchange market, why is it likely that UK interest rates will rise?

3 Your branch is in an English cathedral city, visited by many foreign tourists, and with a thriving industrial estate with several major exporting companies.

(a) What sort of bank products would your branch sell to these two markets?

(b) What would be the effect of a substantial fall in sterling against all major currencies on these two markets and on local shopkeepers and ordinary people?

4 Bearing in mind that oil is priced in US dollars and that we still import heavy crude from the Gulf and export our lighter crude, what effects would be caused to your bank's operating costs (i.e. the general level of prices in the UK) by a substantial fall in the exchange rate of sterling against the US dollar?

5 One of the major exporting companies in Question 3 has been taken over by a US multinational, paying cash to the UK shareholders. What are the effects on the UK's balance of payments? What are likely to be the effects on the company's UK bankers?

6 For what reasons is sterling likely to depreciate against the world's leading currencies?

7 What are the ways in which a country can *correct* a deficit on the current account of its balance of payments?

8 What are the ways in which a country can *finance* a deficit on the current account of its balance of payments?

9 If sterling were to rise substantially against the world's major currencies, what effects would this have on:

(a) exports of UK manufactured goods?

(b) profits remitted from overseas subsidiaries and branches to their UK parent companies?

10 Oil is priced in US dollars. If sterling were to rise against the US

dollar, what effect would this have on the sterling price of North Sea oil?

11 Why do branches have to 'book a rate' with their foreign exchange dealers before accepting a large order from a customer? Would it be necessary to 'book a rate' if the exchange rate were fixed?

12 When the oil price rose for the second time, in 1979/80, the UK was producing substantial quantities from the North Sea. Dealers promptly marked up sterling, so that it appreciated against most other currencies. What effects would this rise have had on our exports of manufactured goods?

13 Do many customers of your branch have deposits denominated in foreign currencies?

14 Estimate how much of your monthly pay goes on imported goods or goods manufactured in the UK under licence from a foreign company. Include savings for your annual overseas holiday.

15 If sterling were to fall against the DM and the yen, but remain unchanged against the Italian lira and the Spanish peseta, how would this affect your monthly budget?

16 Find out from your bank's annual report and accounts what percentages of its profits/income and/or deposits/advances are denominated in foreign currencies or derived from international banking rather than domestic banking.

17 Explain what are meant by *nostro* and *vostro* accounts. Why cannot a bank sell international banking products if it has no nostro accounts?

18 Explain what is meant by 'purchasing power parity'.

19 Why are interest rates so important in determining foreign exchange rates?

20 Why are British exporters of manufactured goods opposed to sterling rising too high against other currencies, as might occur if oil prices were to rise substantially?

10
Government

1 Objectives

When you have studied this chapter, you should:

1 be able to distinguish between fiscal policy and monetary policy and know where they inter-act;

2 understand what is meant by the PSBR and the vital significance of the source of the borrowings;

3 understand what is meant by 'the monetary counterparts' (to changes in M3);

4 be aware of the wide range of the Bank of England's operations, and, in particular, of how it affects the commercial banks;

5 be fully aware of the differences between monetary policy and the prudential regulation of banks;

6 know how monetary policy is implemented;

7 know in outline the prudential controls imposed on banks by the Bank of England.

2 Introduction

We came across government intervention in the economy in Chapter 4, in respect to evening out the business cycle, and also in Chapter 3, when we looked at monopolies and mergers. Here we examine in greater detail, first fiscal policy and then monetary policy. The Treasury and the Bank of England work closely together in these matters and the term 'the authorities' is used to describe them. Finally, we study in broad outline the prudential controls imposed on banks by the Bank of England.

3 Fiscal policy

In Chapter 4 we saw that fiscal policy is one weapon which a government can use in attempting to stabilise the rate of economic growth. It involves the use of government expenditure, taxation and borrowing not just to carry out the functions of defence, education, transport and health but to affect the whole economy. The questions asked when the budget is prepared are not 'How do we finance this expenditure?' but 'How much expenditure should be undertaken in order to keep economic growth and inflation within their targets?' and 'How should this expenditure be financed so as to help to achieve the target?'.

The latter sub-divides into:

1 'If we are to change taxation, then which taxes and which tax rates should be altered?'
2 'If we are to increase borrowing, then should we raise our finance from banks, from the rest of the domestic private sector or from overseas?'

In nearly every year, the government spends more than it receives in taxation and other income such as NHS charges. This *budget deficit* is financed by borrowing from banks, from people and financial institutions and from overseas, and the accumulated debt arising from this borrowing is known as the *national debt*.

But economists are interested not just in activities of central government, i.e. the ministries in Whitehall, but also in those in other parts of what is known as the *public sector*, i.e. local authorities and the remaining nationalised industries. Local authorities and the public corporations which run the national-ised industries receive grants from the central government, they can borrow from the central government and the local author-ities levy taxes in the form of rates on private and commercial property. In the early 1990s it is possible that the rates will be phased out and replaced by a *community charge* levied on people rather than land and buildings. A more down-to-earth name for the community charge is *poll tax*. There could be a political storm over these proposals which, fortunately, do not directly concern the banks significantly, because they and other business will continue to pay rates.

However, fiscal policy does involve the banks because:

1 they pay taxes on their profits, and rates on their branches and other buildings, thus reducing their cash flow;

2 their customers pay taxes, thus reducing their cash flow;

3 the manner in which taxes are paid and the dates of the payments can be important because banks provide the payment mechanisms. If payments are all made on particular days, e.g. early January, then these can cause shortages of liquid assets as balances at the Bank of England are run down to pay the government;

4 as we shall see later in the chapter, fiscal policy can affect monetary policy, especially the level of interest rates (because the government is such an important borrower), and the banks are directly affected by monetary policy.

3.1 Public sector borrowing requirement (PSBR)

A shortfall in income can be financed by either:

1 increasing liabilities, i.e. borrowing;

2 running down assets, i.e. selling assets or drawing upon cash balances.

These options are available to individuals and firms, as well as to governments.

In fact, the UK government is selling a large proportion of its assets, by privatising some of the nationalised industries. This is unusual, and governments normally finance their excess of expenditure over tax and other income by borrowing. The *PSBR* is a term devised to monitor this borrowing, and it *includes not only the central government's borrowing but also that of local authorities and the remaining nationalised industries.* The figure is net of borrowing *between* the components of the public sector, because local authorities and nationalised industries do borrow from the central government.

The PSBR's importance for banks is not so much why the borrowing is occurring as who is providing the finance. If the government borrows from the private sector rather than the banks, from what is termed *the non-bank private sector*, bank deposits fall as the government receives the borrowed funds and then rise again as it spends them. In the first instance, bank deposits fall along with the banks' balances at the Bank of England, but the government's expenditure subsequently restores both to their former levels. The effect on bank deposits and, of course, on the money supply, is nil and this applies whether the borrowing is in the form of sales of gilt-edged securities to NBFIs or of national savings securities to ordinary men and women.

However, if the government borrows from the banks by issuing Treasury bills, the effects are very different. The first round effects are purely on the banks' assets, as they lose bankers' deposits and receive Treasury bills in their place. But when the government spends the money which it has borrowed, bankers' deposits at the Bank of England rise, as do the bank deposits of the private sector. Bankers' deposits are restored to their former level but Treasury bills and bank deposits are higher.

3.2 Medium Term Financial Strategy (MTFS)

This was announced in 1980 and comprised a rolling target for the PSBR and various monetary aggregates for up to three years ahead. While the authorities would probably argue that the single target of M0 which exists in 1987 is in keeping with the spirit of the MTFS, there is no doubt that their thinking has moved towards monitoring other targets (but not in public) and, especially, the exchange rate. The fact that inflation is now much less than it was when the MTFS was announced will be cited as evidence of the strategy's success.

4 The monetary counterparts

These are the 'contra' entries to an increase in the money supply, which is usually taken as being M3.

They form an identity, which should be learnt very carefully if you go on to Stage 2 of the Banking Diploma, and you need to know the counterparts to M4 as well. However, for the Banking Certificate you should merely be aware of the nature of the various 'contra' or 'counterpart' items.

We saw earlier that if the PSBR is financed wholly by sales of gilts to the non-bank private sector then there is no change in the money supply. However, it is purely a fluke if this occurs and, in any case, we have to take into account the bank deposits created by bank lending.

Accordingly, we begin with these three statistics and then take into account the overseas sector. The latter can lend sterling to UK residents who deposit it in UK banks or bank advances in sterling to UK residents can be switched into foreign currency and deposited in banks abroad. A surplus on the current account can lead to a rise in the money supply; a deficit to a fall. Finally, we take into consideration the fact that some of the increase in the PSBR and in bank lending may have as its 'contra' an increase in the banks' non-deposit liabilities, i.e. capital and reserves, and not in bank deposits.

The expansionary influences are:

(a) PSBR;
(b) extra bank lending in sterling to the UK private sector;

These are neutralised if they are accompanied by

(c) government debt sales to the non-bank sector;
(d) an increase in non-deposit liabilities of banks;
(e) changes in the external transactions which mean UK private sector bank deposits have fallen.

Table 10.1 1985/6

		£bn
PSBR		5.8
Increase in bank lending to private sector in sterling		21.5
		27.3
Less	Sales of government debt to private sector	−3.6
	Increase in banks' non-deposit liabilities	−2.0
	External and foreign currency counterparts	−2.6
Change in M3		19.1

The components of M3 rose as follows:

	£bn
Notes and coin in circulation	0.5
UK private sector sterling sight deposits	10.0
UK private sector sterling time deposits	8.6
	19.1

So we add a + b and then take away c + d + e. This should give us a figure which is the increase in the money supply (which is taken as M3). What we've done is to add the two major sources of funding for an increase in bank deposits (borrowing by the government and the private sector) and then take away the contra items which are not increases in bank deposits. The final item – the external transactions – can either increase or diminish sterling bank deposits, but here we are treating it as diminishing them.

In the 1985/6 financial year, which ran from 1 April 1985 to 31 March 1986, the statistics were as in Table 10.1

5 The Bank of England

The Bank of England is the UK's central bank and stands at the head of the banking system. It was founded nearly 300 years ago, as a joint-stock bank at a time when joint-stock companies were granted royal charters. In 1946 it was at the top of the Labour Government's list of private companies to be national-ised, having become a central bank by historical development.

Like other nationalised industries, the Bank is not a govern-ment department and its employees are not civil servants. The Bank's role is to work within the framework of government, to contribute to the policy-making process and to implement that policy when agreed. This work is undertaken at a series of meetings at various levels between officials of the Bank and the Treasury, culminating with meetings between the Chancellor of the Exchequer and the Governor. Almost certainly the personal-ities of the Chancellor and the Governor must have some effect on the relations between the Bank and the Treasury.

5.1 The Bank's functions

These are many and may be grouped into operational and advisory. However, as the monetary and financial markets be-come more complex and as innovative new products are launched, some of the Bank's functions become more difficult. We shall see later how one monetary target (M1) became distorted when banks began to pay interest on current accounts and such changes make the implementation of monetary policy not an easy task. Moreover, rapidly changing markets and new finan-cial instruments increase the difficulties for the Bank in ensuring that firms in these markets act prudently rather than recklessly.

Operational functions

1 It is responsible for the note issue.
2 It provides banking facilities for the central government and for banks.
3 It issues gilt-edged securities to help finance the PSBR.
4 It acts as registrar of the national debt, maintaining the lists of stockholders and paying the interest on the due dates.
5 It executes monetary policy.
6 It operates in the money markets, partly to help finance the government and partly to execute monetary policy. It is in the discount market that it operates as 'lender of last resort'.
7 It operates in the foreign exchange market, intervening from time to time to influence the exchange rate, and manages the official holdings and gold and foreign exchange reserves.
8 It supervises the banking system.
9 It oversees the financial system, in particular the securities (stock exchange) and commodity markets.

Advisory functions

1 It is a link between the government and the City, but it does not act as a speaker for the City.
2 It collects a great deal of statistics, which help to provide a background for its discussions with the government to formulate policy.
3 It analyses the UK economy, and its forecasts also provide a scenario for its discussions with the government.
4 It has assumed an industrial liaison role, arising from the tribulations of UK industry in the early 1980s. Its branches, in Birmingham, Bristol, Liverpool, Manchester, Newcastle and Southampton, are very active in discussions with business people to assess such matters as cash flow, profitability and export competitiveness.
5 It maintains relations with overseas central banks and international institutions such as the IMF, the World Bank and the Bank for International Settlements (BIS). The BIS is a unique bank, being a sort of central bank for central banks, and monitors the Euro-currency markets throughout the world. Surprisingly, because it is located in Switzerland, a non-member of the EEC, the BIS also undertakes work for the EEC.

The Bank of England affects commercial banks directly when it carries out its prudential regulation of them. They are affected indirectly by its operations in the discount and foreign exchange markets. In the discount market, it affects their deposits and liquid assets, as well as the levels of interest rates. In the foreign exchange market, the Bank's operations affect the commercial banks' liquid assets, but, more importantly, they affect the exchange rate of sterling. This affects the profitability of their international business.

5.2 Organisation

The Bank is managed by a court, comprising the Governor, Deputy Governor and sixteen directors. Of the latter, four are full-time and twelve part-time; all are appointed by the prime minister for four years. The Governor and the Deputy Governor, however, are appointed by the prime minister for five years.

The Bank is organised into five groups:

1 *Operations*, comprising the Banking and Registrar's Department and the printing works.
2 *Corporate services*, providing support services to the other four groups.
3 *Banking supervision*, responsible for supervising some 600 banks within the terms of the Banking Act 1987. We will examine prudential regulation later in this chapter.
4 *Finance and industry* monitors the financial problems of industrial companies. It played a particularly important role in putting together 'rescue packages' for distressed firms in the early 1980s under pressure from a high exchange rate, high interest rates and high inflation. Also under this head is a division concerned with the securities and financial markets generally.
5 *Policy and markets* comprises a number of divisions:
    (a) *Gilt-edged*, responsible for operation in long-term government securities;
    (b) *Money markets*, responsible for operations in the discount market and monitoring events in the sterling 'parallel' markets;
    (c) *Foreign exchange*, which operates in the foreign exchange and gold markets, where it can intervene on its own behalf or on that of other central banks, to support sterling or another currency;
    (d) *The territorial and international divisions*, which report on economic trends throughout the world and maintain contacts

with most other central banks and international organisations. In particular, it liaises with the IMF and the World Bank.

(e) *The economics division* specialises in the analysis of the UK economy and produces the Bank of England Quarterly Bulletin.

6 Monetary policy

This seeks to ensure through the financial system that the government can achieve the *economic aims* which we studied in Chapters 4 and 7. The authorities cannot influence gdp or unemployment directly so they seek to control what are known as *intermediate targets*, such as the money supply, bank advances, interest rates and exchange rates. In order to reach these targets, the authorities use various *instruments* such as open market operations. In the past, these instruments have included portfolio constraints such as special deposits, levied on banks, as well as ceilings on bank advances and guidance to banks on priority categories for their lending. By 1987, all these portfolio constraints had been discarded, so they will be discussed separately.

6.1 Intermediate targets

In the period 1979–87 there have been a considerable number of these targets. M3 was a target from 1979 to March 1987, under its old name of sterling M3. Since then, there has been a single target, M0, which had become a target in 1984, when it replaced M1. M0 contains no interest-bearing current accounts at all and comprises mainly notes and coin outside the banks, together with some of the banks' balances with the Bank of England. The authorities considered that the growth of interest-bearing sight deposits, or current accounts as the public calls them, was affecting the reliability of the statistics. Customers were leaving large sums in these accounts, not to buy goods and services, but to buy and sell stock exchange investments.

It is understood that the authorities are watching many of the aggregates which were outlined in Chapter 7, but they are committed to a published target on only one, M0. For the financial year April 1987 to March 1988 the target is an increase of between 2% and 6%. A new target will be announced in the 1988 budget and, of course, other indicators may be chosen to be targeted.

The most important development in the mid-1980s has been the gradual rise in importance of the exchange rate as a hidden, unpublished intermediate target. The authorities could have established targets for the sterling against the US dollar, the DM and the yen, as well as perhaps a figure for the sterling index. Observers believe that, in the summer of 1987, the authorities were unofficially pegging the sterling to between DM2.95 and DM3.00 to £1, possibly in preparation for the UK's full membership of the EMS. However, if the UK undertook the obligations of such membership, it would not be able to use the exchange rate as an intermediate target of monetary policy.

Another possible target for the government is the growth of *money gdp*, that is the growth in the output of goods and services as measured by current prices and before offsetting for the rise in prices across the whole economy. If money gdp grows too fast, this could be because *real* gdp is growing too fast, as the economy peaks, or because prices are rising much faster than real gdp. Or, it could be any combination of these two causes.

6.2 Instruments of monetary policy

Interest rates

Until 1971, the bank rate of the Bank of England was a major instrument of monetary policy. It was the minimum rate at which the Bank would act as lender of last resort to the discount market, and was penal in that it was above market rates and the loans were usually for no less than one week. Every Thursday morning the Bank announced the bank rate for the following week, but in times of crisis it could be raised at any time. In 1971 it was superseded by the *minimum lending rate* (MLR), which was calculated weekly by a formula to give a rate slightly higher than the average rate at the Treasury bill tender for the previous Friday. MLR was abandoned in 1981, although it was re-introduced for one day in January 1985, when sterling was under pressure. In the mid-1980s interest rates were used with a view to curtailing the growth of domestic credit as well as to the needs of managing the exchange rate. You will recall that in Chapter 6 we noticed how the personal sector is borrowing approximately as much from the banks as it is depositing with them.

Since 1981, the Bank of England has operated a much more flexible interest rate policy. Every morning it publishes its estimates of whether or not the discount market will need help from it in meeting its net payments to the government. The estimates are revised several times during each day and the Bank provides any help needed by buying bills in one or more of four bands. The first band comprises bills with 1–14 days to maturity, the next 15–33 days, then 34–63 and the fourth is 64–91 days. (91 days is approximately three months.)

The rate at which these purchases are made is the best signal of the Bank's wishes for the future course of interest rates. A sudden sharp rise, such as occurred in early August 1987, will cause the retail banks to raise their base rates.

Open market operations
Traditionally these took place in the gilt-edged market or in Treasury bills in the discount market. However, as we saw in Chapter 5, the major assets in the discount market are commercial bills and it is in commercial bills that the Bank of England now conducts its open-market operations.

The Bank has several ways in which it operates:

1 it can buy the bills outright from the houses;
2 it can use a *sale and repurchase agreement*, under which it buys the bills but under which the houses also agree to the Bank selling the bills back to them at a later date, often when the Bank expects there to be a surplus of funds. This surplus could arise from the government paying substantial amounts in interest on a gilt-edged stock or from Milk Marketing Board payments to farmers.
3 it can lend directly to houses, against the security of bills or CDs, but usually for no longer than seven days.

In the gilt-edged market its primary concern is to ensure the steady financing of the PSBR from the non-bank private sector, i.e. the NBFIs in the main.

Reserve requirements
These play a very minor role as an instrument of monetary policy, certainly when compared to the 12½% reserve asset ratio of 1971–81. Banks above a certain, small size are required to place 0.45% of their eligible liabilities as non-operational non-interest-bearing deposits with the Bank of England. Because these deposits are non-operational, they do not appear in the statistics for M0. *Eligible liabilities* are, broadly, a bank's sterling deposits from non-banks with an original maturity of two years or less.

Over-funding the PSBR

It should be noted that the practice of *over-funding the PSBR* ceased in the autumn of 1985. Under this practice the government borrowed from the non-bank private sector more than it needed to finance the PSBR. This created great pressure on the banks' liquid assets when the borrowings were paid to the government, which had no intention of recycling the money back to the private sector by spending it. The Bank of England acted as 'lender of last resort' by buying vast quantities of commercial bills from the discount market. These bills, held by the Bank, were christened the 'bill mountain'.

Since 1980 there has been much less reliance on fixed rates such as MLR and a high reserve ratio for all banks for the operation of monetary policy. The authorities have become more flexible in their approach and use their judgement to a greater extent. This not only places a burden on the authorities but it also makes studying more difficult for students, who have few concrete examples or formulae to read in their textbooks. However, this flexibility and the use of a single published target, i.e. M0, in place of two or three, is more in line with a market-oriented economy than the rigidity of the late 1970s and early 1980s.

6.3 Brief history of monetary policy

To counter the recession in the 1930s, interest rates were kept very low and this policy was maintained during the second world war (a 3½% war, Keynes called it, in contrast to the 5% of the first world war). When interest rates rose in the 1950s, banks faced losses on their fixed-interest gilt-edged securities. During this period great attention was paid to a 30% liquidity ratio for London clearing banks which was reduced in 1963 to 28%. Special deposits were first called from the clearing banks in 1960 and extended to all banks in 1971. The 1950s and 1960s were the era of qualitative controls, with Bank of England guidelines on lending by banks and with minimum deposits and maximum terms for HP. Personal loans from banks were subject to similar controls to those published in statutory instruments for HP companies.

In 1971 a document called 'Competition and Credit Control' introduced a 12½% reserve asset ratio for all banks, so clearing banks were not handicapped by a 28% ratio in competing with non-clearers not subject to this ratio, which affected their cost of funds and hence their profitability. The clearing banks agreed not to link their interest rates to Bank rate and to publish their own base rates. Unfortunately, the 1971 changes did not distinguish clearly between monetary and prudential controls and the Bank of England failed to monitor the secondary banks and their excessive lending to property companies (as did the Department of Trade and Industry). A wit remarked that there was 'too much competition and not enough credit control'. The economy boomed, oil prices rose dramatically, as did interest rates. To restrain bank lending, punitive supplementary special deposits, nicknamed the *corset*, were introduced on interest-bearing deposits. In 1981, the 1971 provisions were rescinded and a second new era began with very few portfolio constraints.

Questions will *not* be asked in the examination on these events, but they have helped to influence the thinking of today's decision-makers. If the political complexion of the government should change, there may be a demand for the re-introduction of some of the old techniques.

7 Prudential regulation

This is now completely separate from monetary policy and is designed to ensure that banks are not only financially viable, i.e. solvent, but are seen to be so by their customers. It ensures that banks act prudently rather than recklessly. One cause of the increased emphasis given to prudential regulation since 1973 was the secondary banking crisis which came to a head early in 1974, when the Bank of England had to enlist financial support from the clearing banks to prop up failing secondary banks, of which perhaps the most notorious was London and County Securities. These secondary banks had lent too much of their deposits to ailing commercial property companies and, when interest rates virtually doubled in under a year, banks in the inter-bank market marked down their limits on these secondary banks which could not repay their inter-bank deposits as they fell due for repayment.

A second cause of the interest in prudential regulation was the UK's entry in the European Community, because the Community required a more formal approach to bank regulation. Accordingly the Banking Act was passed in 1979 and divided banks into two: *recognised banks* and a more restricted category of *licensed deposit takers*. The Act was repealed in 1987.

7.1 Banking Act 1987

This came into operation on 1 October 1987 and replaced the 1979 Act. Just like its predecessor, it was born out of a crisis, i.e. the failure of Johnson Matthey Bankers, which was attributed to the two-tier system created by the 1979 Act. It is not a charter outlining the powers and duties of banks, but provides the statutory basis for the Bank of England's existing supervision of banks and continues the existing deposit protection scheme.

Its most important provision is that the business of every *authorised bank* must be conducted in a prudent manner. Each authorised bank must:

1 have adequate capital and liquidity;
2 make adequate provision for depreciation and doubtful debts;
3 maintain adequate accounting and control systems.

The Bank of England judges the adequacy of these criteria for each bank, not in relation to rigid ratios but with regard to each bank's individual circumstances.

The Bank of England approaches the first two of the criteria by looking at the contra items in each bank's balance sheet. Thus, when assessing capital adequacy and the adequacy of provision for depreciation and doubtful debts, which are found on the liabilities side of the bank's balance sheet, it closely examines the bank's assets and the degrees of risk attached to these assets. When assessing the liquidity of a bank's assets the Bank scrutinises the composition of that bank's liabilities and, in particular, the relative shares of wholesale and retail deposits and the currencies in which these deposits are denominated.

New banks, before they are authorised by the Bank of England, must have paid-up capital and reserves of at least £1m and, if they are to include the word 'Bank' in their name, this total must be not less than £5m. There is now a right of appeal if the Bank refuses authorisation. A tribunal will be appointed for each appeal, with a right of appeal to the High Court on a point of law.

The Act has also established a *Board of Bank Supervision* to to oversee the banking supervisory operations of the Bank of England. It comprises three members from the Bank, i.e. the Governor, Deputy Governor and the executive director responsible for banking supervision, and six independent members.

7.2 Other legislation

In common with all financial institutions, banks are subject to the provisions of the *Financial Services Act 1986*. It affects them, not in their core banking business, but mainly in connection with the way they sell their non-funds based products such as life insurance policies and unit trusts. Each bank and building society has had to decide whether to deliver only its own products or to drop its own products and sell those of other institutions and thus rely solely on commission rather than management fees and profit. Most banks have opted to deliver only their own products, although some trustee branches are selling a wider range, but Nat West has decided to be the odd one out and consequently has had to sell its unit trust operation (it never had a life insurance subsidiary). Most building societies, however, have chosen to sell products from many suppliers, although the Abbey National has elected to sell products from only one supplier, Friends Provident, a leading insurance office.

The *Consumer Credit Act 1974* is largely outside the scope of this book, and parts of it will be studied in 'Banking: the Legal Environment'.

7.3 Other protection

This includes the *Deposit Protection Fund*, which guarantees 75% of each customer's protected deposits with a bank, up to a maximum protected deposit of £20 000. Every bank contributes to the Fund.

Personal customers in dispute with a bank may ask the *Banking Ombudsman* to resolve it. The Ombudsman, who is a lawyer appointed by a council of the 18 banks, is empowered to make an award of up to £50 000 in each case.

The government can refer proposed mergers between banks to the *Monopolies and Mergers Commission* which can also investigate other market situations. It investigated the 'duopoly' between the rival Barclaycard and Access credit card networks some years ago but they are now (1987) the subject of a further reference.

Summary

Fiscal policy is concerned with taxes, government spending and borrowing (PSBR). If government borrowing is to be non-inflationary, then it has to borrow from outside the banking system, from you, me and our pension funds.

The monetary counterparts show arithmetically how much of the increase in the money supply is due to the PSBR and bank lending, after allowance is made for government debt sold to non-banks and for other factors.

The Bank of England works within the framework of government and its functions can be grouped into operational and advisory. Perhaps its two most important functions are to advise the government on economic policy and to implement monetary policy once it has been decided.

Monetary policy operates through the financial system, whereas fiscal policy also operates through the spending of government departments. There is one published monetary target – M0 in 1987 – and probably undisclosed exchange rate targets. The major instrument of achieving this (these) target(s) is a flexible interest rate policy together with several techniques of operating in the discount market.

Prudential regulation is now separate from monetary policy instruments and is based largely upon the Banking Act 1987.

Questions

1 Assess the effect on the UK's economy if interest rates were to rise substantially in:
   (a) the USA;
   (b) the Irish Republic.

2 How is liability management facilitated by the existence of wholesale money markets?

3 Which are the three main sources of finance for the public sector?

4 'The Bank of England's most important role today is to act as *prudential* controller of increasingly *innovative* financial markets'. Explain the words in italics and also list other important roles of the Bank.

5 'The government is such a large borrower that it affects the level of interest rates in the discount market. Therefore, there is no perfect competition in the discount market.' Explain.

6 What is meant by the term 'parallel money markets'? Why are they important to commercial banks?

7 'The Bank of England can either control the supply of money or its price, i.e. interest rates. Like other monopolists, it cannot control both.' Explain.

8 Monitor the development of EFTPOS, *electronic funds transmission at the point of sale*. What other products do banks sell to help their customers make payments within the UK?

9 Explain what is meant by MV = PT and classify some of the banks' main products as to whether they:

(a) help to finance T;

(b) facilitate V;

(c) are based upon M.

10 '*M1* and other measures of *narrow money* seek to assess how much money is being supplied to meet the *transactions demand for money*.'

(a) Explain what is meant by the three terms in italics.

(b) Explain how the growth of interest-bearing current accounts is making M1 less reliable as an indicator of transactions balances.

11 List the various liabilities of banks and classify them into those which are money and those which are not.

12 Explain how gdp is calculated by the expenditure approach. What bank products help to finance this expenditure on the gdp?

13 Thirty years ago a bank instructor told his class: 'Banks have three main functions: they pay, receive and transfer money, they lend money and they have a range of miscellaneous services.' How true is that summary today? In what ways have the functions of banks changed, if at all?

14 What is meant by the term 'quasi-money'? Why does it not include the liabilities of banks?

15 Your manager has asked you to give a short talk to a group of business students on 'How the banks finance businesses'. Make a list of the various ways in which banks do this, to help you give the talk.

16 Your manager has asked you to give a short talk to a group of business students on 'How the banks finance exports and imports'. Make a list of the various ways in which banks do this, to help you give the talk.

17 Compare and contrast how banks help to finance the gross fixed capital formation of:

(a) companies (in plant, machinery, buildings, etc.);

(b) people (in new houses).

18 'XYZ plc reports interim results next week, which are likely to reflect the impact of a weaker dollar, as 50% of the company's earnings now come from the USA.' This sentence, from the FT, assumes that readers know whether profits are likely to be up or

down as a result of the dollar's weakening. Explain, in everyday language, how a weaker dollar will affect the profits.

19 Your manager has asked you to talk to a group of GCSE students on 'Money in a modern society'. List the headings you would use to help you give the talk.

20 Have you enjoyed studying the course?

Appendix

Economics and the Banks' Role in the Economy

Specimen Paper 1

Time: 3 hours.

Answer 5 questions. All questions carry 20 marks: marks for sub-sections are shown in brackets.

1 What is meant by the term 'perfect competition'? [10]
To what extent does it exist in practice in any of the wholesale financial markets, including the foreign exchange market? [10]
2 Define the term 'elasticity of demand' [7]
How is it measured? [7]
 Would you consider the demand for your bank's travellers cheques to be elastic or inelastic with regard to the commission charged in their sale? Give reasons for your answer. [6]
3 Distinguish between commercial banks and building societies. [14]
 Why are there over 500 offices of banks in the City of London (EC postal districts) but less than 50 building society offices there? [6]
4 What assets usually act as money in a modern economy? [6]
 Why do governments control the supply of most (if not all) of these assets? [14]
5 Explain the difference between nominal rates of interest and real rates of interest. [8]
 What effects may high positive real rates of interest have on
 (a) retail banks? [6]
 (b) their commercial customers? [6]
6 Examine the likely effects, if any, which a rise in the exchange rate of sterling against all major currencies might have on:
 (a) the UK tourist and travel trade (for both home and overseas holidays);

(b) the UK motor manufacturing industry;

(c) UK commercial banks with branches in overseas countries.

7 Distinguish between:

    (a) balance of trade;   [4]

    (b) balance of payments on current account;   [4]

    (c) balance of payments on capital account;   [4]

Give brief examples of products by which banks facilitate and profit from international trade, payments and capital movements.   [8]

8 As part of the preparatory work for a course at your bank's training centre you must compile a report on an aspect of the local economy in which your branch operates. Show how a new factory, employing 2000 workers (recruited from the pool of local unemployed), could affect the local economy and hence the business of your branch.

9 What are the essential features and functions of a central bank?

Specimen answers 1

1 Perfect competition is said to exist when:

    (a) there are a large number of buyers and sellers;

    (b) there is freedom of entry into and out of the market;

    (c) no one buyer or seller is large enough to affect the price as a result of their purchases or sales.

In effect it means that sellers can sell as much as they wish at the market price.

In the wholesale markets condition

    (a) applies;   [3]

    (b) does not apply, because Bank of England approval, in one form or another, is required for entry. Departure could involve loss of face and, moreover, a downgrading from a 'bank' to an 'LDT';   [3]

    (c) applies only in part, because the Bank of England does not act as 'lender of last resort' (and thus influence interest rates) and also can intervene to support the exchange rate.   [4]

2 Elasticity of demand measures the extent to which the quantity demanded changes as the price of the product changes. Generally it is negative – sales decline as price rises.

It is calculated by dividing the percentage change in the quantity demand by the percentage change in the price. If this is greater than 1 (strictly >1) then demand is said to be elastic; if less than 1 (<1) then it is said to be inelastic.

Likely to be elastic, i.e. a 1% rise in commission would cause sales to drop by more than 1%, because there are a large number of substitutes (our competitors' travellers cheques).

3 *Commercial banks* are engaged in accepting deposits and, most important, lending for a wide variety of purposes. Some provide money transmission services (clearing banks). Wide range of other products. Supervised by Bank of England and, mostly, limited liability companies.

Building societies are mutually owned, accept deposits (usually called 'shares') but lend almost exclusively at present for house purchases by owner occupiers. They will become more like commercial banks soon, especially now that the Building Societies Act has been passed. Some will become limited liability companies.

Both banks and building societies are located to serve their markets. The City of London is one of the world's largest financial centres and hence there are so many banks there. Building societies, however, serve mainly the personal market, so that 50 offices suffice for the people who work in the City and for the deposits which they attract from solicitors and companies located there.

4 Coin, notes but, above all, bank deposits. To some extent building society shares and National Savings Bank deposits act as 'quasi-money'.

It is argued that the total of money in a country can influence the level of output either by people spending it directly or by the money supply affecting the level of interest rates, which in turn could cause entrepreneurs to invest more in capital equipment and thus have multiplier effects on output.

5 Nominal rates of interest are expressed purely in money terms e.g. 5% per £100 pa, and take no account of the changing purchasing power of the principal sum borrowed. Real rates of interest take this changing value into account (it is usually downward, as a result of inflation) by dividing the nominal rate by the inflation rate (usually a simple subtraction will suffice). Thus an 8% nominal rate with inflation at 3% a year is a real rate of interest of +5% (strictly +4.85%). When inflation exceeds nominal interest rates, real interest rates become negative.

(a) retail banks are not directly much affected by high positive real rates of interest, but they are indirectly affected by the fortunes of their customers. Because banks make a 'turn' on what they lend they can use the real rate of return in their lending to build up their capital base.

(b) Non-banks have to repay more, in terms of purchasing power, than they borrowed, with deleterious effects on their profitability. Thus, business failures would rise and banks would have to make greater provision for these bad debts.

6 (a) Inward tourist visitors would decrease, as the UK became a more expensive country. UK holidaymakers would go abroad in greater numbers, as the £ bought more units of foreign currency. Fewer UK citizens would holiday at home.

(b) Exports would tend to decrease as UK cars cost more in foreign currency but, more important, because exports are small compared to imports, imports would increase.

(c) All amounts expressed in foreign currency would fall when converted to £, so that overseas profits (unless rising more rapidly) would fall in sterling terms.

7 (a) Exports fob – imports fob.

(b) Balance of all current transactions – visible and invisible (dividends, services etc).

(c) Net long-term capital flow – especially government loans, portfolio and direct investment.

By Forex deals, travellers cheques, letters of credit, collections, guarantees and bonds, negotiations, barter and counter-trade, forfait, ECGD credits, SWIFT, Eurocurrency syndications, Eurobonds.

8 Such a new factory would have considerable multiplier effects

(a) via the initial construction;

(b) via the workers spending their wages locally.

Stress should be made on the leakages – to other towns, to government and through savings.

The branch, even if it did not get the account of the factory, should benefit from increased deposits, loans and fee-based income. Increased home loans and personal loans should be a marketing target.

9 Textbook answer.

Specimen Paper 2

Time: 3 hours.

Answer 5 questions. All questions carry 20 marks: marks for subsections are shown in brackets.

1 What is meant by the term 'oligopoly'? [5]
To what extent does it apply to:
  (a) the UK retail branch networks of the clearing banks? [5]
  (b) the production of motor cars in the UK? [5]
  (c) arable farming in the UK? [5]
2 (a) Tourism is regarded as having a 'high income elasticity of demand'! Explain what is meant by this statement and then show how your bank has developed a range of products to take advantage of this situation. [10]
  (b) What is meant by the term 'joint demand'? Why are credit facilities so often available at large retailers? [10]
3 Distinguish between monetary policy and fiscal policy. How are commercial banks affected by a government monetary policy?
4 Why do people wish to hold money? [12]
What products have the banks developed to satisfy this need? [8]
5 Outline the essential features of:
  (a) discount houses; [7]
  (b) merchant banks; [7]
  (c) building societies. [6]
6 Following the loss of substantial subsidies from central government, bus fares in Northtown, with a population of 600 000, rose last month by 60%. Examine the possible effects on:
  (a) the number of passenger journeys made; [7]
  (b) the bus company's total receipts in Northtown; [7]
  (c) the demand for personal loans from banks for customers to buy motor cars. [6]
7 Describe how the UK commercial banking system has been affected by mergers over the past 20 years.
8 What are the principal factors affecting the supply and demand for sterling in the foreign exchange markets?
9 You are the second officer in a small branch, whose manager is away on sick leave for a fortnight. He has asked you to deputise for him at a chamber of commerce open forum on the likely effects in the town's local economy of a reduction in the basic rate of income tax to 25%, given that unemployment in the area is currently 16%.
  Would you speak in favour or against this proposal, and why?
  Would you prefer more government expenditure in your district rather than a reduction in income tax?

Specimen answers 2

1 A market with from 3 to 7 suppliers, such that a price reduction by one of them is likely to cause the others to follow suit, as market shares are lost. A price rise, however, is likely to cause sales to drop away unless there is strong consumer loyalty or external factors (such as inflation, common labour or resource costs) which cause competitors to follow suit. Consequently, there is great emphasis on product differentiation and brand loyalty.

(a) Quite typical of retail banking – numbers of supplying banks, price changes and marketing strategies.

(b) Typical of motor car manufacturing, except for powerful overseas competition, but this in turn is also oligopolistic in nature.

(c) Not typical. Prices are set by the EEC and no one farmer can affect the price.

2 (a) Income elasticity of demand relates the quantity of a product demanded to the income of consumers. As consumers' real incomes rise, so the amount of tourism they buy rises faster. Hence we have an increasing demand for second holidays, bargain breaks, and winter holidays, as well as more overseas holidays.

The banks' products include credit cards, Euro-cheques, travellers cheques, foreign currency tills.

(b) Joint demand occurs where one product needs another to complement it or to facilitate its consumption – e.g. bread and butter, cutlery and crockery, the purchase of a durable good and finance/insurance for it.

Credit (and hire purchase) is demanded by customers in order to buy the goods, so the retailer is merely supplying the customer needs.

3 Monetary policy involves:

(a) the stocks of financial assets and liabilities – money supply, bank advances, hire purchase, commercial paper etc.;

(b) the level of interest rates;

(c) the exchange rate.

Fiscal policy involves public (central and local government and nationalised industries) expenditure, revenue and borrowing. It can affect monetary policy but only the best students are likely to make this point.   [10]

Commercial banks provide a large part of the money supply and their advances are their most profitable assets. Hence their profits will be affected by changes in deposits and advances, as well as by interest rate changes. If the banks take new positions in the foreign exchange markets or have large revenues in foreign currency then exchange rate changes will affect their profits.

4 Transactions, precautionary and speculative motives. Best candidates may mention permanent income by hypothesis.

(a) *Transactions*: cheques, credit cards, current accounts

(b) *Precautionary*: 7-day deposits, term deposits, high interest cheque accounts

(c) *Speculative*: links with gilt-edged 'market makers' after the 'Big Bang', unit trusts.

5 (a) Nine small houses acting as a 'buffer' between central bank and commercial banks. Dealing in Treasury bills, gilts but, most important now, in the commercial 'bill mountain'. Closely supervised by Bank of England.

(b) Sixteen 'acceptance houses' plus a larger number of other merchant banks. They advise, deal in the markets, but their balance sheet totals are relatively small compared to those of the commercial banks. Closely supervised by the Bank of England.

(c) Mutual organisations, very closely linked to provision of home loans for owner occupiers, but moving into commercial banking in recent years. Building Societies Act is likely to accelerate this move. Supervised by the Building Societies Commission.

6 (a) Sixty per cent rise in fares could lead to at least a 30% drop in journeys made. Short journeys would be more affected than longer ones,

(b) On the above figures, receipts would rise – demand is inelastic.

(c) One would expect personal loan requests to rise, but not as much as the drop in bus journeys.

7 Mergers of late 1960s to form Big Four.

Links with overseas banks – 1981 Standard Chartered and Hong Kong & Shanghai attempting to buy Royal Bank of Scotland; 1986 Lloyds tries to buy Standard Chartered; 1986 'Big Bang' many banks merging with stockbrokers.

8 *Supply of £*

Supply of £	Demand for £ (increase of supply)
Imports	Exports
Capital outflows	Capital inflows
Dividends and other invisible payments	Dividends and other invisible receipts
Hot money chasing higher interest rates overseas.	Hot money chasing higher UK interest rates.

9 Need for new employment and the multiplier effects on local trade. Will this be outweighed by the extra spending generated by a cut in basic income tax?

Difficult to say but most local business people would probably prefer government expenditure to an income tax cut, because the benefits are more easily seen.

Best scripts will mention the need to be tactful, since we are representing the bank.

Index

Accelerator 55
Accepting houses 67
Addictive goods 9
Advances 93, 110
Age distribution 10
Agriculture 35–6, 117
APR 78
Authorised banks 164
Authorities 151
Average costs 29–30, 32

Balance of payments 112, 124–32, 141
Bank of England 66, 156–65
  exchange rate policy 146, 160
  functions 156–8
  lender of last resort 73, 160–1
  origination 158–9
  signals on interest rates 80, 161
Bank for International Settlements 157
Banking Acts 163–4
Banking Ombudsman 165
Banks 65–100
  advances 93, 110
  American banks 67
  asset management 94–5
  assets 90–4, 99–100
  balances with Bank of England 91
  base rate 74–5, 80
  capital 87–90
  cash 91
  central bank 66
  clearing banks 41, 80
  consortium banks 67
  corporate market 81, 98–9
  deposits 66–7, 106–8, 110–12
    sources 98–100
    foreign currency 147
  foreign exchange risk 146–7
  inflation – effects of 52

Banks (cont'd)
  international business 123−4, 132
  investments 92−3
  Japanese banks 66
  liabilities 86−90
    contingent 94
  liquid assets 90−1
  merchant banks 67
  personal market 81, 98−9
  premises 93
  Profit and Loss Account 96−7
  prudential regulation 147, 163−5
  retail 37, 39, 66−7
  savings banks 67
  special deposits 94
  unemployment 60−1
Barometric price leadership 42
Base rate 74−5, 80
Baskets (of currencies) 144−5
Big Bang 81
Board of Bank Supervision 164
Brettonwoods 143
Building societies 41−2, 69−70, 80, 95, 165
Building Societies Act 30
Bureau de change 91, 138
Business cycle 56−62

Capital 4
  share capital 87−9
Capital account of balance of payments 126−37
CAR 79
Cartels 41−2
Certificates of deposit (CDs) 73
Cheques 92, 103
Circular flow of income 53
Command economics 61
Commercial bills 72
Commercial paper 74
Comparative advantage 118−20
Competition and credit control 41
Composite rate of interest (CRT) 79
Concentration ratios 37
Consumer Credit Act 78
Consumers' expenditure 54, 56
Costs 29−30
Credit cards 82
Cross elasticity of demand 24
Currency baskets 144−5
Current account 124−32
Custom 9−10
Cyclical unemployment 59

Debt, problem 147–8
  service 127, 128–9
Deflator 47
Demand 8–11
  joint 24
Deposit Protection Fund 165
Devaluation 129–30
Diminishing marginal utility 9
Direct investment 126, 131
Discount market 36, 72–3
Diseconomics 33
Disintermediation 69, 74, 112
Division of labour 31–2
Domestic credit expansion (DCE) 108
Dominant firm price leadership 42

Economic goals 61–2
Economics – definitions 2–3
  language 3–4
  how to study 4–6
Economies of scale 32
Effective demand 8
Elasticity of demand/supply 20–4
  manufactured goods 120
Eligible liabilities 91, 161
Endowment element 80, 87
Euro-commercial paper 74
Euro-currencies 147–8
European Currency Unit (ECU) 145
European Economic Community (EEC) 1, 3, 42, 121–2, 163
European Monetary System 145–6
Exchange control 61, 122–3, 129
Exchange rates 23, 129–30, 136–47
  fixed and floating 142–4
Expectations 141
Export controls 10, 122
  promotion 129–30
Exports 54, 124–30
External assets and liabilities 126

Factors of production 5
Fair Trading Act 37, 42–3
Fashion 10
Financial intermediaries 55, 68–70, 98–100
Financial markets 70–4
Financial Services Act 165
Fiscal policy 62, 152–6
Fisher, Irving 113
Fixed costs 29
Fixed exchange rates 142–4, 146

Fixed interest securities, price and rate of interest 92, 109
Floating exchange rates 142–4, 146
Foreign exchange market 36, 136–48
Frictional unemployment 59
Functions of money 104

Gearing 88
General Agreement on Tariffs and Trade (GATT) 121–2
Gold price 143
   standard 142–3
Goldsmiths 94–5
Government 12, 42–3, 49–50, 61–2, 79, 111, 151–4, 159–65
   borrowing from banks 111, 154
   influencing RPI 49–50
   monopolies from non-banks 111, 153
   taxation 12, 19, 152
Gross domestic product (gdp) 5–6, 52–6
   gdp deflator 47

Habit 9–10
Horizontal integration 33
Hyper-inflation 50

Import deposits 122
Imports 54, 56, 124–30
Income 2
   effect on demand 9
   elasticity of demand 24
Index linking 51
Index of retail prices (RPI) 47–50
Indicative planning 62
Industrial and commercial companies 98–9
Inflation 50–2
Insurance companies 68–9
Inter-bank market 73
Inter-company market 74
Interest elasticity of demand 24
Interest profits and dividends (IPD) 125
Interest rates 74–80, 112–3, 140–1, 160–1
   base 74–5
   composite 79
   exchange rates 140–1
   LIBOR 75, 80
   MLR 160
   monetary policy 160–1
   nominal 77
   real 77
   theory 112–3
   true 78–9
   yield curve 76
Intermediate targets 159–60
Intermediation, financial 55, 68–70, 98–100

International Monetary Fund (IMF) 126, 142, 143
International trade 117–24
Investment 3–4, 54–5, 126–7
Invisible exports 125–6, 132

Keynesianism 114

Labour 4
Land 4
Lender of last resort 73, 160–1
Limit pricing 41
Liquid assets 90–1
Liquidity 90
Local authority market 73
Location of industry 32–4
London – Inter-bank offered rate (LIBOR) 75

Managed flexibility 143
Margin 4
Marginal costs of funds 77
  costs 29–30
  product 12
  propensity to consume 56
  returns 12
  utility 9
Market 8, 30–1, 34
  clearing 14–15
  economics 61
  makers 37
  share 6–8
Markets, financial 70–4
  corporate 81
  personal 81
Medium term financial strategy (MTFS) 154
Merchant banks 67
Minimum lending rate (MLR) 160
Mixed economics 61–2
Monetarism 114
Money 103–15
  characteristics 104
  creation 110–2
  definition 104
  demand for 108–9
  functions 104
  history of 105
  role of 113–5
  supply 106–8
Monetary aggregates 106–8
Monetary counterparts 154–6
Monetary policy 62, 159–63
Monetary policy instruments 160–2
Monopolies and Mergers Act 62

Monopolies and Mergers Commission 42, 165
Monopoly 40–3
Multiplier 56
Multinationals 95–6, 138

National Savings Bank 67–8, 81–2
Nominal rate of interest 77
Non-bank financial intermediaries (NBFIs) 68–70
Notes and coins 91, 106–8

Offshore banking centres 147
Oil price 142
Oligopoly 38–9, 79
Ombudsman 115
OPEC 41
Open market operations 161
Opportunity cost 29
Organisation for Economic Co-operation and Development (OECD) 1
Overfunding 162
Overseas sector 98–100, 111–12

Pension funds 69
Perfect competition 34–6, 79
Personal sector 98–99
Petro-dollars 148
Phillips curve 59
Population 10
Portfolio investment constraints 126, 131
Precautionary demand for money 109
Price 8–24, 47–52
   discrimination 40
   leadership 40, 42
Private sector 98–9, 110
Product, marginal 12
Prudential regulation 163–5
Public sector borrowing requirement (PSBR) 153–5, 162
Purchasing power 42
Purchasing power parity 142

Quality legislation 122
Quantity theory 113–4
Quasi-money 105
Quotas 122, 129

Real rates of interest 77–8
Reserve requirements 161
Retail banking 37
   deposits 94–5
   financial markets 70–1
   prices 47–50
Returns, diminishing marginal 12
Rights issue 89
Lord Robbins 3

Savings 3–4
Scrip issue 89
Seasonal unemployment 59
Second (communist) world 1
Secondary banking crisis 163
Securitisation 81
Services 125
Smith, Adam 31
Special deposits 94
Specialisation 30–4
Speculative demand for money 109
Spread 139
Stagflation 59
Sterling commercial paper 74
    index 145
Stocks, changes in 54, 56
Stores, competition for banks 82
Supply 11–13
    elasticity 24
    joint 24

Take-over code 43
Tariffs 121
Taxation of goods 12–3, 17–9
    of bank interest 78–9
Technology – effect on supply 11–2
Third world 1
    debt problem 147–8
Transactions demand for money 109
Transfer payments 53–4
Treasury 151
Treasury bills 72, 91, 111, 160
'True' rates of interest 78–9

Unemployment 58, 120
Unit of account 104
    use of US dollar 125–6
Unit trusts 68–9
US dollar 142, 143
    as unit of account 125–6
    major Euro-currency 67, 147
Utility 9

Variable costs 29
Velocity of circulation 113
Vertical integration 33
Visible trade 124–5
Voluntary export restraints (VERs) 122

Wholesale financial markets 71–4
Work-in-progress 54, 56

Yield curve 76